THE MORTICIAN

BC Bentley

JONES MEDIA
PUBLISHING

Jones Media Publishing
10645 N. Tatum Blvd. Ste. 200-166
Phoenix, AZ 85028
www.JonesMediaPublishing.com

Disclaimer:

The author strives to be as accurate and complete as possible in the creation of this book, notwithstanding the fact that the author does not warrant or represent at any time that the contents within are accurate due to the rapidly changing nature of the Internet.

While all attempts have been made to verify information provided in this publication, the Author and Publisher assume no responsibility and are not liable for errors, omissions, or contrary interpretation of the subject matter herein. The Author and Publisher hereby disclaim any liability, loss or damage incurred as a result of the application and utilization, whether directly or indirectly, of any information, suggestion, advice, or procedure in this book. Any perceived slights of specific persons, peoples, or organizations are unintentional.

In practical advice books, like anything else in life, there are no guarantees of income made. Readers are cautioned to rely on their own judgment about their individual circumstances to act accordingly. Readers are responsible for their own actions, choices, and results. This book is not intended for use as a source of legal, business, accounting or financial advice. All readers are advised to seek services of competent professionals in legal, business, accounting, and finance field.

Printed in the United States of America

ISBN-13: 978-1-945849-83-1 paperback
JMP2019.2

CONTENTS

CHAPTER ONE

SPRINGTIME IN THE WESTERN HEMISPHERE is the season each year the beginning signs of renewed life appear. Winter across the States can range from mild to frigid and fierce deep freezes. Wherever I have lived, and for as long as I can remember, springtime is my most adored time of year, and as each new day begins with the sound of songbirds in the early morning to wake me up, I excitedly open the windows and doors to welcome the new, fresh air after having windows closed for so many months. From morning to night, Mother Nature is always aggressively at work with mother birds hard at it making new nests, signs of new plant life just about everywhere, trees beginning to bud, and people are up sooner to get out and enjoy the outdoors before the summer sun requires us to close the house up again to run the AC.

The days get gradually longer, winter wear gets packed away, and out come the sandals, shorts, and dresses. Workouts and tanning begin ahead of shaping plans for vacations, outings, and get-togethers amongst friends and colleagues. People are the happiest and most active this time of year, with strong and clear ambitions to make memories, *this year is really going to count* thoughts, perhaps check off some of the bucket-list ideas. But, without a DOUBT, those plans and accomplishments are where a clear majority of romance novels, music, poems, and movies steal material from. It is a time when our most creative sides unfold, dreaming becomes a daily pastime, and it all comes naturally! Colors and styles are seen just about everywhere, new fashions hit the runways, new trends, social media use increases, life is so active and loud, running aligned with the universe, and comes with two choices: be dedicated or be left behind. Everyone knows meeting new people requires change in self, change routines, finding new hobbies to enjoy with others, joining a group, checking out the online seen, local events to increase your possibilities and visibility of finding new friends, dates, and maybe a significant other. One of the best places for beginners is places with continual changes filled with continual options, is the gym for working out, because everyone is there with the same goal in mind—transformation. The gym is a great place for conversation, partner activities, groups, and a place to release stress.

So, while the biological clock ticks on, the gym can feel very natural for your physical and mental transformation, just until the wedding invitations start to arrive, or the graduation announcements, and suddenly we are right back to how NOT to be the only single person again, and solving it goes right to the top of the "to do" list. The single person begins evaluating everyone they know and their situations to try to compare and analyze their own situation. Staying up late at night trolling social media for some sort of hint or scanning the faces of those who claim happiness, but their faces say different. How long has it been for me? Is my run of bad luck over, or am I just cursed?

★ ★ ★

I was laying on the couch watching a movie one evening by myself with the front door open when several cars come in a caravan down the street, pulling into the parking spaces up and down my street. Once stopped, their doors flung open, music blared, and it was like clown cars the number of people who crawled out of them laughing and talking as they headed to a party down the street from me. I sure do remember those days in my youth, being one of the crowd. I have been so busy building my career I had forgotten all about making a life for myself or having fun. I started thinking about my current situation and how I should be sitting here with my girlfriend, or maybe my wife, or out for the evening at the movies, maybe with other couples doing "couple things"—or better yet, on vacation! I certainly should not be sitting here alone on the couch by myself peeping out the front door or window watching the world go by…

Just about then an infomercial came on the television about busy professional singles seeking other busy professional singles online. It was almost like the stars lined up perfectly for me, considering all the current events going on at this very moment, and this big hand pointed right at me to get my butt out of the house and out meeting someone new! Get out with a group of people, into the crowd. Just like the visitors on my street.

I've seen these infomercials before, heard them on the radio, at the bus stop, pops on social media—a huge assortment of ways to meet other people and get involved. "Are you single?" This specific one on the television tonight I have seen plenty of times, and by some sort of statistic, the marketing group must be cornering or tapping into the busy professionals and entrepreneurs category to know running this ad at this time, on a Friday night, a higher number of busy professionals (like me) are home sitting alone watching TV desiring a personal life change or a significant other. The timing and place was just right for me, sitting on the couch while the carloads of people twenty feet from my front door funneled into the streets. I definitely perked up watching the infomercial, paying more attention to the testimonials, and wouldn't you know it, my buddy and his wife popped up on the screen as one of the successful couples! I had no idea they met online. I never asked, but this seemed far too coincidental, but it definitely piqued my interest as a sign of a potential life change was on the way.

I pulled up my tablet and logged onto the website, checking it out. I texted my buddy and he confirmed he and his wife met on the site several years ago. It seemed encouraging, but before I took the plunge I wanted to read some more recent reviews. I looked through platforms for searches, and it had four and five-star reviews just about everywhere I looked. I spent several hours reading and searching, unable to find anything negative about the site I was considering joining. The more I read, the more I got encouraged to try this—or was I talking myself into it? I have read and heard a lot of horror stories over the years, and when it comes to matters of the heart I tend to be very guarded. I read there is a multi-step process the site uses to assure personal safety and concealment of identity to assure people who were joining the site were real people and not phishing bots for advertising agencies. Only after the multiple-step matching process is complete, cross-compared to a national database, profiles are run through multiple algorithms, will my personal information be shared with the other person who also passed the verification process. The testimonials stated if a person goes back and changes answers the flawless system catches it, runs the algorithm-matching system again, and matches you again with the best possibilities. I was still pretty uncertain until I read millions of other likeminded professionals and entrepreneurs who work 85% of the time have little time to build a personal life. SOLD, SOLD, SOLD!!

I started to enter my sign-in details, and quickly paused again to self-evaluate my life to assure myself once again this is what I wanted? Was I ready to jump right into this? I started to type again and found myself in a long, deep thought process comparing myself to many people I know from all walks of life. Gosh, how am I already in my early 40s and the only one I know with no kids, no oopsies, no abortions, no divorces, and no drama? I actually do have a remarkable life, well-traveled, all my finances sorted, homeowner, cool cars, well dressed, low stress, business owner, a beautiful home, very healthy, all the possessions a guy could want, an awesome dog, no drama... And, according to all the health and wellness articles, I am the model individual. Why would I want to screw it all up, become like all the people I know, jump into the piranha pit and swim with alligators entering the online singles world? Sounds like an Indiana Jones adventure to me, and I am going to find the most precious artifact. The only thing I hope for is it doesn't belong in a museum! Oh, I laughed out loud about that. Let me continue with at least signing up and get a free view of what the site has to offer.

CHAPTER TWO

I RECEIVED MY CONFIRMATION EMAIL and signed into the site with my new credentials. I took a long look at everything as I browsed throughout the entire site, and found it to be very encouraging—lots of testimonials, pictures, wedding pictures, dating advice, events, speed dating. It was impressive, and the potential women I saw really encouraged me to keep moving on this. I read testimonials why people joined the site, and they were identical to what I felt, and more I had not even thought of. I found comfort the same problems and thoughts existed in all age groups, all the way into late 60s, all due to being a dedicated professional. There were chat rooms, activities, crisis centers, online counselors, blogs, articles, statistics—they had everything to help anyone. I felt very comfortable knowing I was not alone, and thousands of people from all around the country heavily into their careers share the same as I do.

I took matters into my own hands, jumped into my personal profile, and made a dedicated choice to put all my finest efforts into this project of myself, and I was going to meet someone special and make this work. I am committed to changing and bettering my life by finding my partner in crime, my soulmate, getting on the path of finding love and enlightenment. The first one-third of the questions were about what I would expect from a dating site, starting with my basic stats like how tall I am, my age, body type, color of my hair... Then onto my current situation, such as, am I single, separated, divorced, widowed, in an open relationship, etc. Then it asked me if I was heterosexual, or any part of LGBTTQQIAAP, and I just paused, wondering what I was signing up for. I probably sound pretty vanilla being a single white heterosexual male looking for a single white heterosexual female! Boy, I must have been living under a rock! After about three more hours and about two-thirds the way through the first 200 multiple choice questions designed especially for the site's most advanced algorithm matching system, the last third was repeated questions, just words resorted to ask a different way. The questions up to this point were very in-depth, many not even dating questions, such as, have I ever driven in snow? Do I prefer tap water or bottled water? If I found a wallet with money in it what would I do? (*I'd take the money and turn it in to lost and found, lol.*) Seriously, what foundations do I donate to have anything to do with meeting someone? Or do I sleep on my right side, left side, back, or stomach have to do with who I might meet? Must be some sort of scientific thing? I know nothing about how all these answers get sorted into a database and out pops a list of the most suitable individuals for me. The only comforting aspect to me is everyone else is doing it too, so it "must" work! It was very redundant and boring, but when I finally made it to the last question the next screen popped up with a party going on, playing parts of Celebration by Kool & the Gang! That was the best part of the whole thing! Whew, it was FINALLY done. Let the matching begin!

CHAPTER THREE

I WAS FILLED WITH THOUGHTS of excitement as I was making moves to better my life. It was enjoyable thinking about having dinner with someone other than a colleague or potential new customer. Thoughts of the most divine dinner with my mystery dream woman would be in the most amazing ambience in about 20 different scenarios as I juggled the ideas around in my head. I was going to really woo her with a dinner on a balcony facing the ocean with a mild breeze, or on a patio with a grand piano playing just for us, next to a fireplace, most definitely with white linen, candlelight, the finest silverware, and the freshest seafood, fine wine, fresh fruit...

I can imagine watching the candlelight reflection in her eyes and off the reflective silverware as I stand and bend over to kiss her on the forehead because we are so much in love. I was not interested in dating a bunch of different people at once, only one. A busy successful professional, just like me, who has her own money, own home, who is independent, and no children so we can spend our time with just each other, putting each other on a pedestal. She too will be first and foremost just as goal-oriented as me, supportive, driven, equal amounts of a listener and talker, trustworthy, great in bed, interested in taking things slow, always smells good, enjoying the friendship and fun times together with no expectations, living in the honeymoon stage for as long as we possibly can to allow the commitment to grow into a beautiful relationship. Vacations, holidays, family, Christmas, kissing under the mistletoe. The perfect relationship is now in reach, and I am intoxicated for the romance, the plans, holding hands, cuddling, a kiss in the morning before work and greeted at the front door for a kiss of hello. I won't be the only single guy in the couples events anymore. I will be with my PIC (partner in crime), a future worth counting on, along with someone to share my deepest secrets, and theirs with me. How bizarre would it be that my significant other is living less than a half a mile away and is laying in her bed thinking the same things as I and just waiting for our introduction. Sweet dreams!

The next morning, I awoke to a woman lying in my bed staring at me with big, full, beautiful blue eyes. I laid there completely content in a trance, staring right back at her. She said, "Don't leave me," and I just kept eye contact with her, wondering what she meant. I suddenly realized who it was, and I frantically jumped out of bed like a hot spring. Nobody was there. It was her again...

Eight years ago, she never made it home, we never got a chance to say goodbye, and she still visits every single time I am about to make a change in my life. It is always the guilt that stops me. She was great, I swore I would never move on without her—until today... It was finally time. I decided I have lived with the guilt long enough. I am healed, I am ready, she is never coming back, and nothing is going to stop me this time. I felt a sense of empowerment, so I marched out into the front room and moved the furniture to the way I always wanted it, instead of the way she had left it. You see, she died that night, and denying my own rule of how to force change into your life is to live like you already have it. I have officially entered the manifestation process to attract the life I always set out to have. The pause button was on for eight years, and I invested all my time and efforts into my health and my career. The only change I've noticed is more gray hair.

I sat down, lit a smoke, and grabbed my tablet, typing in the website to launch my profile to let the matching begin! I was on a mission to attract the woman and the life I have always dreamed of. My mouse hovered over the activate button. All I could see was her big blue eyes filled with crocodile tears looking at me, while the other side of me was chanting "DO IT!" I closed my eyes anticipating seeing my new extensive list of professional, beautiful ladies waiting for me. I did it… I clicked activate. I opened one eye to see them, and instead the next page was about uploading my pictures and instructions to write my own profile in my own words. This will be a cinch, I am already a great writer (smirk), so I wrote an amazing profile, spending several hours to make it just right. I uploaded several pictures of myself doing my favorite things, a cleaned-up picture and a casually dressed one. I re-checked all my work, sent it in for review, and it came back approved within a few minutes. I was so excited. I tapped back over to the activate button and let'r rip!

I didn't even wait to see if something showed up right away. Instead, I closed up my laptop and swore not to look until morning. I laid back down in my bed, dreaming about the possibilities. How will I be able to sort out the number of single women looking for a guy like me? Just the fifty-mile radius around me is four million people. I wonder how far away she will live from me? My head was unhitched from my daily life, and I was dreaming again. It has been so long. I was so excited thinking about the possibilities beside the daily work grind. What does she do for work? Scratch that thought… What kind of house? What kind of family? Where will we go to dinner? What kind of movies does she like? The questions rolling around my head were endless. I looked over at the clock, already 4am, so excited I can't even think about sleep. I rustled around in my medicine cabinet to find a sleep tonic… NyQuil, expired two years ago… I took a swig—gross… That stuff never tastes good. I fell asleep thinking of tomorrow. What will it bring?

CHAPTER FOUR

IT'S SUNDAY MORNING AND I awoke just after 10am, and just like every other morning I reached over to grab my phone, and it said I have 99+ new emails. Whoa, what?!?! Extremely excited, I ran over to my laptop, signed in, and it said 1,007 new emails. WOW! I guess my phone maxes out at 99, and then I heard my phone ding again, so I checked it and it was still at 99+, so I refreshed my page, and my email is up to 1,012. Five more already? I thought to myself, *Why didn't I join this thing 6 months ago?* Just then another ding, the responses were pouring in! I was so proud of myself. No blue eyes in the bedroom this morning, things seem to be foraging forward the right way, so I decided to not open my email. It really felt great to be a sought-after man, and so many single ladies are out there looking for a guy like me.

My whole frame of mind and my day suddenly changed. It was not my typical schedule, etched in stone how I was going to get ready for the work week. I felt like I was walking on cloud nine. I hopped in the shower, and my typical five-minute shower was a super soaker today to process exactly the right kind of woman I would want. How I will sort through each one? I will be kind and genuine to each one for sure. I always have other's feelings in mind as a priority, so I will show them good men still exist, and the ones I am not interested in I will let down slowly and gently. I feel a little bad, but I feel good! I wasn't sure exactly how I was going to balance my work life since it pretty much consumes every aspect of my daily routines, but I really look forward to telling my customers I have a personal life now.

I hope she will be supportive rather than demanding of my time with ultimatums, and I will be of her too. It will be casual, a friendship, and go slow, just as it was always intended to be. I know I want a brunette, shorter than me, one or two kids are ok, no cougars—I have a friend who is only forty and she is already a grandmother, so no grandpa status for me yet! I am a hound dog for home cooking, so I would really like to meet a woman who is a good cook vs a microwave genius. She is comfortable in her own skin, comes from a good family, college educated, oh…paints her nails, that is so hot! A nice build, athletic, medium sized boobs—not a mandate, just preferred—likes animals, is frugal, wait… All that was in the long questionnaire, I guess I was just practicing with myself, but as the list is growing I know people will say just about anything when it dawned on me it is probably why that system asked questions a couple different times in different ways. Wow, that is smart! I went in to check my email again, and now it is over 1100. GEEZ!

I almost clicked to open it. I could feel my hand tingling, but nope! I was going to savor this moment. I was needed just as badly as I needed one of them. This is so awesome to feel wanted. I just kept planning out skits in my mind as I went on with my day, having conversations with myself exactly how it would play out in different scenarios. Like when I went to get some lunch and playing like holding hands. Opening the door for every lady I saw—and being thanked felt great. Maybe one of those is her. My phone kept dinging away all throughout the day, but it was worthless to even look at it. 99+ was the best it was going to get. I will check it when I get home. I took a long drive. I was in dreamland all day. I treated myself to a nice dinner and thought about how the last eight years I put everyone else first instead of myself, seeking approvals.

I was so riddled with guilt after the love of my life tragically passed away, time just got away from me, and she always visited whenever I was about to do something, so I felt cursed. Broken-heart pain lasts a long time, but today I learned it lasts only as long as you allow it. I forgot all about being a human being, I felt undeserving, when the truth is being a human is all about moving forward. Receiving the number of messages that I received today tells me there are mountains of people just like me wanting to move forward and are willing to put their foot forward to start new beginnings. I was very encouraged by the day's events, and the time to open my email to sort through the details was about here. I took the long way home from my last destination and articulated my plans in my head step by step, exactly how and what I was going to do leading up to the final moments before I open the new chapter of my life. This is one of the biggest events I can recall for a very long time. Eight years are coming to a close, and this will be the first step towards my new life. When I finally arrived home, I followed my plan exactly. I put myself first. It was a sweet torture, but my time was set for 9pm I would log in and feast my eyes on my new life. I watched my regular shows, and for some reason I was the leading part in all of them. All the shows were about romance, breaking up, starting new lives… It was kind of crazy, everything seemed to be just for me. I did lose track of time watching the shows when suddenly my alarm went off at 9pm. I felt kind of a pit in my stomach, I was intimidated and excited all at once, but it was finally time…

CHAPTER FIVE

I SAT DOWN IN FRONT of my computer, logged in, and to my surprise I saw 2,126 new emails. I just felt kind of a buzz about it, the whole day and everything up to now just rushing through my veins like an adrenaline rush. It was the moment of truth. With a drum roll in my mind, I entered my log-in credentials, put my mouse over the log-in button, closed my eyes, and clicked. Every single message in big capital letters was **SPAM** WHAT THE… I haven't had more than ten spam messages a day in ten years, and I have over 2,000!!! No, no, no, no, no. NOOOO!!! The email messages were everything from Russian brides, women in the Ukraine, car polish, meet hot singles in my area looking for sex, big-busted women, pay off my student loans, some African estate I was part of and the receiver of multi-millions of dollars… I clicked on one of them. It said I answered blank on a questionnaire, and in response I received this! The algorithm matching system was a spam bot!

My junk folder was even bigger, with over 12,000 messages in one day! Flowers, coupons, credit scores, lower my bills, life insurance… What in the HELL!? I clicked my spam filter and delete all, and had a whopping two emails left, one from my mother, the second from a client. There was not a single response to my profile in over 200 pages. THAT'S what the whole questionnaire was about! The website is a scam! How in the world am I going to be able to run my business with all this crap filtering into my email box daily? I was so livid I went right to the website, steaming to complain. I was going to get my money back and report them to the FCC, FTC, and APWG.

As soon as I logged in the main screen said I had 37 reviews of my profile…. I guess I felt a little better momentarily, and in the bottom right hand corner in very small gray font it had a disclaimer I never saw before that said, "WARNING!!! We are not responsible for excessive email or spam messages that may be forwarded to your personal email box." I know in the IT industry this is perfectly legal. Still upset, I went ahead and looked at the 37 people who viewed my profile. I was locked into the membership services for at least thirty days. Yes, the website does take advantage of people who are looking for love—I suppose it pays the bills. I felt totally scammed and speculated the 37 views were just click funnels to drag me in deeper into the system. I was totally against the thing at this point, but I kept processing the success stories and my beautiful day I had with myself and how great it felt, so I decided to go ahead and look at my viewers.

I clicked to view potential matches, and I could tell at least half of them were scammers based on the pictures and backgrounds. I had enough of it, the hype was gone. I started to log out when I suddenly received a live chat request. What is this? Another scam? It crossed my mind that maybe the trick to this is I needed to be logged into the site for the thing to work? I went ahead and looked at the woman tagging me for a live chat session, and she was very attractive, the background was a pink designer background, maybe it was glamour shots? She didn't live far from me, she loves animals, likes to cook at home, comes from a large family, has light brown hair, dressed well, a casual picture, her profile read well, and the message popped up in the middle of the screen again saying "Hello, are you there?" I was VERY hesitant, but I went ahead and replied. She wrote back, and we started talking in a chatroom style.

The system would say she was typing, and when I typed it had a notification I was now typing, it was neat. It was my first time in a chatroom like this. She was very nice, a great conversationalist, funny, and we shared many similar ideas and liked many of the same things. The conversation went on for a couple of hours, and I really enjoyed it. There were no dead moments, she had a witty personality, she was down to earth. It was definitely not artificial intelligence talking back to me, or a computer-generated system to keep me online, she was a real person! This wasn't so bad. I asked her to take this offline and she quickly obliged. We exchanged telephone numbers, and as soon as we did, we were right onto text messaging. We didn't miss a step. It felt very natural, and we talked that first night for five hours, until after 2am. I quickly forgot all about the online fiasco.

I guess it wasn't so bad I had to go through all that riffraff to be reminded out of everything bad comes something good. While I was texting with her, I managed to log back onto the website and redirect my emails to a junk email address I have (always more than one way to skin a cat…). We ended the night's conversation agreeing we would continue it the next day. When we had a final goodbye, I was appeased. She was just like me! I was excited and looking forward to hearing her voice and hearing her laugh. So far she has passed all the tests and met my traditional requirements—she was shorter than me by a couple inches, she owned her own house, she had her own career she followed out here from the Midwest, she has pets and she likes others, she also sometimes works nights and weekends—as I do—she has been single for several years, she was not seeing anyone right now, AND she had exactly the same thing happen to her with the boat load of emails just like I had. SHE WAS AWESOME!!! I asked her when she would be able to meet, and she answered perfectly: she said she wanted to take things slow (smiles). She said to date she has been on the site for about a year, has been on several dates, and people lie about their appearance, put up very old pictures, and are not who they say they are. She was done with the online things, and I was her last hope. This really made me feel like gold. "Always save the best for last."

My original plan to woo her was really set to launch correctly. She said my profile spoke right to her heart, and she knew I was one to put effort into it. She also really liked the written part of my profile and asked me if I was a writer or just good with words? Things were really lining up perfectly for the perfect launch in my mind. It was the first time in a very long time I connected with someone so well. It was very encouraging. She definitely removed the doom and gloom I had been feeling about what I had signed up for, and where I was preparing myself to have to sort through thousands of women, it felt like more than ever the good man upstairs was winking at me. Life is good!

CHAPTER SIX

BRIAN IS 38 YEARS OLD, born and raised in the Midwest, is six-feet-tall, very handsome, styled, short brown hair, gleaming white and straight teeth, cleanly shaven, and always well-dressed in the latest fashion. Even in his downtime he is dressed to the nines, as he even wears stylish pajamas to bed. He is very athletic and works out about five days a week and is very health conscious. Brian is in the upper-middle class pay range, drives a Mercedes, has great abs, very friendly, comes from a great family, does not have children, but the kids and animals love him. He is always about the details. Brian considers himself always on display, so he even wears great smelling colognes and nice watches. Behind the perfectly chiseled appearance is a hidden secret. He is always working, at times 60-80 hours a week. He always sees things as the glass half full, he is very goal oriented, meticulous, and always willing to lend a helping hand.

Those who know Brian never have anything bad to say about the guy, so what is the driving force to keep a guy so well put together all the time that nothing gets the guy down, or at least seems that way, while NEVER showing his cards?

Brian has often been the center to many rumors of him possibly having a hidden drug problem, or perhaps a gambling addiction, or into the black market, because he is never down, very well dressed, appears to have lots of money, extremely well liked and respected. Everyone often wonders and talks about what his dirty little secrets are or what exactly continues to drive him to be at the top. It is impossible of the human condition for anyone to continually live up to an expectation so great and so mighty he holds it together continually and keeps on doing it day after day. What is he hiding, who pays his bills, what is the secret?

The secret is he was badly hurt in a car crash many years ago and lives in extreme chronic pain. He has two mal-union leg bones, and although his leg wasn't set correctly, between the pain and the deformity he somehow turned a bad injury into an attractive, smooth swagger. Nobody is ever able to tell anything is wrong, and due to the cause of the horrific accident he should not have survived, fired off the gift of the sixth sense. Brian says living in chronic pain around the clock, he continually experiences the gift. He can't turn it on or off, he says it has stayed on since the onset, but not only does it leave an open opportunity for blue eyes to continue to visit, it has taught him pain is the superior power and is the small gap between the living and the deceased. Brian's tall strong stature and perfected appearance is a shield from the grim soul-searching spirits who roam amongst us seeking to harm through pain whether it be physical or emotional. The non-stop pain and severity of his condition is the paranormal dinner bell, so Brian prefers to be surrounded by others to push his stalkers away from clinching to his chronic pain. He prefers to be a model for others to look up to, works continually in an industry in which he always looks like a modern-day superman, and lives happily to push the darkness away. Ultimately, his former lady accepted him the way he was and his love for her kept the grim away, so when she tragically left, her spirit won't leave him to move on. Will his new friend be able to ward the spirits away?

Jennifer, on the other hand, is a tall lady, standing at 5'10". She is the oldest of her siblings and grew up in a large family all very close in proximity. Her grandmother lived across the street, and all the cousins, uncles, aunts, and family within a 50-mile radius. Jennifer used to be a big girl growing up. She was constantly the butt of jokes, teased for her weight and clumsiness, and bullied constantly. Until she reached her height of 5'10" she was a huge sports enthusiast, and her grandmother was her best friend, always by her side, always there for her, supporting her in everything she chose to do.

Outside of the family, Jennifer spent all her time alone. She went off to college and studied an array of different studies deciding what she wanted to do. She spent several years in college changing her major and eventually graduated with multiple degrees. After college she returned to living in the small town, because this is what the family has done for many generations. After a year Jennifer really wanted more than the small town had offer, she wanted a fresh start. She tried to discuss her wishes and plans with her family, however she was mocked and laughed at and therefore denied the family's approvals. She was told to get back home, forget the crazy talk and advised if she left, she would be shunned from the family. Jennifer's mind was made, she had nothing left in the town since her grandmother had passed away, so she cashed in all her bonds, sold everything, saved all her money and headed west. Her first transformation began with getting quite a bit of plastic surgery. She had a tummy tuck, breast augmentation, and brachioplasty. She also had laser vision correction and got the tattoo she always wanted. Jennifer is also very much into fashion and style, so she replaced her entire wardrobe, she has beautiful naturally straight teeth that are VERY white. Since her move and transformation she says she is very well respected and claims her move away from the small town was the best move of her life. She often laughs and says the physical changes she elected run neck and neck for first place with moving away from the small town, but combined her self-confidence is very strong. She has the most amazing emerald green eyes and all the years of college she finally elected a career in fashion and a professional makeup artistry. Her grandmother left her quite a chunk of inheritance money, so she bought a house with cash. Jennifer has two feline fur babies, so the only thing missing from her life was the right man. Her career, just like Brian's, was her life, both of their professions they both work long hours, weekends, and love the clients. Jennifer claims her amazing talents made a quick name for herself and works in a very specialized field. She vacations regularly, has many friends, but like Brian, nobody to call her own.

CHAPTER SEVEN

JENNIFER AND BRIAN QUICKLY BEGAN talking every single day. From opening eyes after sleep they'd greet each other with "Good Morning". They'd continue right on throughout the whole day when they could communicate with texts, voice memos, gifs, memes, pet names, right on into the evenings, through dinners all the way until they both went to bed saying goodnight—

Jennifer and Brian were in continual contact, carrying on about everyday subjects, like best friends typically do. Day after day they created a bond and an expectation to talk at least every hour, and it was very enjoyable even through demanding work schedules. Jennifer is always making Brian laugh! About a month in, they were talking on the phone together on a Saturday night when another car full of kids pulled up and headed up the street to another house party. Jennifer heard the commotion and asked Brian if he had company and needed to go? He just laughed and told her about the kids headed up to a party up the street just like the night that prompted him to join the site they had met on. He reminded her all he wants to do every night is talk to her. She said, "now look at us, 2 old farts falling in love", she laughed and laughed saying there won't be any more of those nights, and she would much rather walk around with a big rubber band around her head glued to her phone to talk to him, so her arm won't fall asleep. Jennifer always made funnies and kept conversation light. Her imagination mimicking the television salesman on late night television infomercials, or recite off movie moments, she always kept Brian laughing. After her rubber band around the head comment, she rolled right on into how they needed to develop the head belt for the no hands phone talking apparatus watching people drive all over town with belts on their heads. Brian could only laugh on the phone at her, which just encouraged her to keep rolling with her charades. Brian said he just lays on his phone, and without missing a beat she responded how they could put both inventions on late night television, following the singles site commercials how we are solving single people's problems with themselves as the testimonial it really works!! The two of them had every aspect of a great start at best friends headed for a relationship. The only part missing was being together in the flesh. The two of them carried on like this for the next three months every day and every night the two of them were building a routine. Jennifer would periodically meet up with her friends while Brian was working late, and Brian would spend time with his friends while she was working a late shift. On the anniversary of their fourth month together, Jennifer told Brian she had a confession she needed to make. Of course, Brian was completely there to support her, listen to her, and mentioned to her whatever it is was he was there to work through it together. Brian always looked forward to hearing from her, she was everything he was looking for in a woman, and the last four months they took things at a speed that worked for them both developing a bond and a friendship tailored to them. Brian was REALLY into Jennifer despite they had not met physically, but each of their work schedules made it difficult. Jennifer knew very well how to keep it going, always playful, flirtatious, supportive, boosted his ego, they shared private pictures with each other, so Brian was worried on one hand what her news might be, and on the other very confident whatever it was, they would get through it together, and hoped she might surprise him to finally meet. What did she have in mind?

Jennifer called Brian at the regular time like clockwork at the same time as always as they have for the last four months (7:22pm). When she called, he always let it ring 3 times for luck and answered "Hellooooooo" with his big deep voice. Jennifer jumped right in beginning with "Brian, for the last four months we have shared all of our innermost secrets, shared the good, the bad, and the ugly, childhood memories, all of her fears, she has not left out a single detail about herself and she felt safe with him." Brian stayed quiet letting her speak as she continued about how they both have supported each other through bad times, tough times, talked through life decisions, laughed until they both cried. She said, "Brian, you are the most patient man I have ever known, you are handsome, strong, I feel like I am walking on air with you in my life, I think about you constantly of where you are, what you are doing, I almost feel like I am diseased as much as I think about you, but nobody has ever been there for her like Brian was" Jennifer said, "My secret is in all of my transformations I am actually a man"... Brian was completely silent on the phone, a long pause of dead silence, he was completely lost for words. Jennifer broke the silence with another one of her hysterical laughs and said, "GOTCHA, but lucky for you I am NOT a man, and I wish we were on live chat because I can only imagine the look on your face must have been priceless", and laughed and laughed. Brian stayed silent on the phone until she was done laughing and said he had thought about her message all day and wasn't too happy with this being just a joke on him. Jennifer replied saying it was just and opener, what she wanted to tell him is she is deeply in love with him. Brian was silent on the phone again.... He heard her say it again "I love you Brian". Brian responded, "I love you too Jennifer". Brian was a bit stuck for words, as she carried on with a fairytale description of their kingdom, they will live in one day. Brian always enjoyed talking to her, so he kept the conversation going, but his mind was filled with the main question, when are they going to meet?

Over the next several weeks Jennifer and Brian's ideal relationship for their mutually busy lifestyles continued. The two of them were in a full-blown relationship for four plus months, and yet they still have not met each other in person. Brian and Jennifer often spoke about their current situation on the go, however whenever a small opportunity presented itself to get together, the both of them agreed they would create the perfect evening together typically and always right before Jennifer was always flying somewhere, or so was he, so the conversations while thousands of miles apart kept the romance going, when inside the same city, the same daily routines continued . Being on call always interrupted the times they were making plans to finally meet and revert to electronica and routines thereafter. Conversations always never ending, picking back up where they left off and continued to the next subject as if no time ever paused between them. Brian finally understood why he was single all the years, however in this current routine "blue eyes" had not visited since he met Jennifer. Perhaps the curse was finally over because Brian had found new love?

Jennifer understood Brian's chaotic self-employed schedule and Brian understood her being on call. Self-employment has its perks, but working all the time and no consistency in a schedule, is typically lethal to relationships. Jennifer and Brian had a very understanding relationship, and although Brian was more persistent in wanting to meet, Jennifer seemed to know it was better to value the moment. For instance, self-employment with on call is like a survivor's game, you eat what you kill, so when the customer calls after normal business hours, they expect to get help immediately. Typical potential partners translate "on call" after hours as "You just aren't important to me", or "I like work better then you." Jennifer and Brian both understood this and they were a winning combination! From the very beginning the conversation of being on call, weekend hours, traveling were all discussed. Whenever the two of them were in a good conversation, the interrupting phone call was no big deal to either of them, so besides having all the bells and whistles most fabulous relationships have, the number one feature they shared was understanding. Hours could pass between and the next conversation would pick right back up where the last conversation ended. Truly the two of them were best friends before anything else, best matched, and the crazy dating system worked. Brian had no idea how many relationships Jennifer had like theirs, but this was his first. She had amazing skills to never let conversations go stale and kept turning the heat up. Their daily conversations took another step up from trying to always impress each other, they turned into unfiltered and straight-up personal, no filters and no judgements. Jennifer always asked the million-dollar questions. She'd ask questions like "Brian would you run naked through a nunnery for one million dollars?" "Brian, would you eat a pile of dog doo in front of a crowd for a million dollars?" "Brian would eat a banana covered in snot?" Brian always replied yes, and she would laugh hysterically! They talked about traveling, family, people, movies, current events, local news, politics, day-to-day personal problems, work, how the day is going, how did you sleep, dreams... Between the daily work routines, their conversations never got old, and it was both of their best times from the incredibly busy rub. Brian was all about Jennifer, and Jennifer was all about Brian. For the first time for both of them, the relationship was textbook natural, and not centered around sex.

Coming up on 6 months Jennifer and Brian's conversations consisted of a committed couple, and yet still have not met in person.

They relied on each other, talked continually, considerate of each other's feelings and put each other as first priority before work, before family, even sometimes before themselves individually. They made long lists of plans together, how their house would be together, their vacations planned 10 years in advance, where they would go, when, how, etc. Holidays were planned and scheduled, which ones would be her years and with her family, alternating holidays year after year with his. They talked about if her family would like him, and if his family would like her, and if they didn't how they would carry on together. How unusual is it Brian and Jennifer know every part of each other's minds, bodies, sweet spots, scars, birth marks, and have never physically looked into each other's eyes or touched one another? The first time will be like two worlds completely merging. ELECTRIC!

They both have participated in long distance relationships, both have had pen-pal relationships, but this one will set new feats for people and falling in love with each other without any physical touch. It didn't matter to either of them, it was beautiful, they had 100% amicable trust, and they redefined the definition of "virgins"! Jennifer by far is who has kept things at a distance, Brian always persists making times to meet. They are significant others, always call each other all the pet names, like sweetie, babe, shnookums, beautiful, main squeeze, etc. There was not one bit of malice, regret, our doubts between them, they both knew regardless of circumstance, they would be together. They had every bit of everything in common and it was examined in detail under a microscope over the last several months. They told each other I love you at least a half a dozen times every day, they watched the same television shows, they liked the same foods and cooked in the same Midwestern and family styles. They shared many similar family traditions, they worked out together on the same machines pushing each other for betterment, cleaned house at the same time together and in the same fashion. These two were two peas in a pot and it is totally crazy they have never actually met. Jennifer thinks they have in a past life. Brian is good with that idea, but thinks it is totally freaking nuts they haven't met in person yet!

Brian has had many long-term interesting relationships with customers across the country, some in other continents for many years and never met. Brian always talks about Jennifer and about their relationship to friends and family, but by now he bets she must sound imaginary. Brian's "spethal" friend! Brian knows she talks about him too, to friends and family. They both sound so happy all the time, and they both have the phone backgrounds of each other. Even in a digital world where most relationships carry on online, for these two being in the same state, and this deeply in love, never meeting in Brian's opinion is quite unusual. He "is" completely infatuated with Jennifer, and has decided the next time they talk, it is time to really talk about when the rubber hits the road. He loves her, but he has decided it is time to meet, and no more exceptions or excuses… it is time!

Brian was terrified, but his entire intent for joining the website originally was to meet someone exactly like Jennifer. Time flies when you are having fun, and they just carried on beautifully until nearly six months had passed. Brian was head over heels in love with Jennifer and he has never touched her. Jennifer and Brian have invested all this time and effort into each other with the intention of building a future together with a comfortable safety zone to exceed all scenarios and matters life can throw out to disrupt things. Together they had a bubble that will just graciously keep them safe and secure. Jennifer is everything Brian has ever wanted in a woman and then some. Jennifer has surpassed even "blue eyes," and it was time to finally meet! It did cross Brian's mind if meeting each other could put an end to them. How could meeting change anything, this is what they have been talking about is their future, ten years from now, and until death do us part? Brian laughs to himself in private about the possibilities of being catfished. Could it be possible? Brian thought about how inactive his sixth sense has been with Jennifer, but then again, he has not been with her physically. Brian knew everything about Jennifer all the way down to how she likes her lotion put on. He knows all her erroneous spots, he knows all her habits, pet peeves. All they have talked about for the last month is yearning their first touch, their first kiss, their first intimate time together and ALL of the provocative details. They talked about making love, lustful sex, sex in the woods, sex everywhere and everything about it. Brian was certain it was time, and as far as the two of them have taken things, and for this long, she should be just as excited as he is.

Brian laid awake for hours thinking about all the times they had planned to get together even for just an ice cream or for lunch, 100% of the time something work related on her end ALWAYS came up. Brian's customers call generally between 10am through 6pm, and emergency calls typically come in after midnight, and the other times can trickle in between 1am- 4am, but it is rare, those times are several hours after Brian and Jennifer hang up each night. With Jennifer it is always a last-minute cancellations. Brian really started wondering why a woman who has kept his attention for nearly 6 months always bails out at the last minute. He felt it really is time to put in the effort into opening realistic conversations about meeting in person. Brian decided from this moment forward, it will be the next step to their relationship, and losing it all was acceptable. No more cancellations without a plan to meet next. Brian is not going to allow another six more months to pass, it is time!

CHAPTER EIGHT

THE NEXT DAY WENT AS usual. Brian and Jennifer talked all day long, and when the evening conversations commenced, Brian started by telling Jennifer something was on his mind. Jennifer responded in a very concerned manner and asking to please tell, she was supportive, and encouraged him to speak openly and honestly. Brian said, "*I had a dream last night we met in person, and I haven't stopped thinking about it since*", Brian asked her how She felt about it? Jennifer played along like she always does and talked up a fantasy of them both riding in on horses in a large open field full of white daisies and butterflies as their horses galloped towards a castle. Jennifer continued in her detailed visualization all the peasants and animals would be bowing as each of them entered a courtyard for them to meet. Brian giggled as always of her fairytale descriptions, but said he was serious about it this time. Jennifer responded reminding him about all the times they have tried already, and work always interferes, otherwise they would have met a long time ago. Brian said, "*Jennifer, the only interference is your last-minute cancellations every single time.*" Jennifer was quiet… Brian expressed how much he feels for her, dreams of her, and doesn't want it to end, but it was time to meet. Jennifer became very soft spoken and hesitant in speaking any words. She was stuttering and finally said, "Brian, if we meet this will all stop, what did I do for you to want to end this and break up?".

Brian kept an even and supportive tone, spoke slowly, requesting to continue the conversation in person. Jennifer withdrew again talking about how much work she had piled up; she was making excuses to avoid meeting once again. Brian remained assertive and encouraging how much he desires her, how much he wants to be in her presence, hold her hand, warmly hug her, place a kiss on her forehead that everything was going to be ok. Jennifer said, "What about the fairy dust, we have to have fairy dust sprinkles", and giggled like always. He could sense she started to come out of her shell, it was working, and she said how much she has always wanted to meet Brian too. Brian's anxiety dropped until she said something unusual. She said, "I have extremely enjoyed all of the time we have spent together, but why would want to throw it all away?" Jennifer was on that path again trying everything she had in her to not meet in person. Brian stopped her and insisted it was the next step in their relationship. The two of them went back and forth for several hours debating meeting until nothing more was to be said about it, the conversation wound down into a long blank uncomfortable moment of silence. Jennifer said, "Brian are you happy to admit you started our first argument?" Brian was silent and said, "*Jennifer, this is the time when no more words are left to be said and we have make-up sex.*" She was silent, so Brian continued to repeat what he did earlier about how much he wants to be with her all the time, how he thought she should take it as a compliment of how he professed his love to her, and wants to spend all of his free time with her.

Jennifer fired back in a strong tone "We DO spend all of our free time together, and all you are doing is complicating things!" She said, "What else is there to know about me you don't already know?"

Brian was lost for words, he ALWAYS knows what to say, but this is the first time he had ever heard her raise her voice. After a few minutes contemplating what to say next he said, "*Jennifer, you are right, I do know everything about you, except one thing. I know how committed you are to your profession, it is very admirable, I know it is what brought you here from the Midwest, but what is it exactly you do for work?*"

Jennifer was silent and deadlocked for words... she said, "I...I, um... I am technically not supposed to talk about it, it is a private profession, my clients are not to be disclosed and there is a certain level of confidentiality I must follow."

Brian was SHOCKED by the answer. Here is his lady he thought he knew everything about, and she knows everything about him, but suddenly there is a top-secret entity he can't know about, and they are supposed to have complete amicable trust? Brian was quietly fuming because what else has she held from him besides this top-secret profession? So, he asked her again, "*What exactly do you do for a living, and what field is it in?* Jennifer was completely silent on the phone again and changed the subject back to what Brian wanted to discuss about meeting in person. Brian didn't want her to feel like he was attacking her, so he patiently waited for her to speak. Jennifer explained she keeps her profession sworn to secrecy because she is bound by several professional business agreements and non-disclosure agreements which makes it hard to talk about. She continued to explain her profession has ruined just about every single friendship, relationship, date, acquaintance, opportunity she has ever had, so with experience being its greatest teacher, she is just not comfortable talking about it. Jennifer said if they get married, she will have to tell him about it because he will be forever part of the top-secret family and finished off her explanation with a giggle.

Brian felt he had pressed enough, and he also knows patience always wins, so he let her know it was ok, and he appreciated her opening up to him at least as much as she did. This was the fourth or fifth time they both became lost for words in just the past week. After a few minutes Jennifer piped up and alerted Brian her clothes were ready to come out of the dryer and she needed to get going. Brian was completely cordial, as usual, she quickly said goodbye and hung up without saying "I love you,". No more conversations took place for the rest of the evening, they both went to their corners, took the gloves off, and both sent a goodnight text at bedtime.

Brian laid awake in bed that night distracted and sidetracked from his normal nighttime duties by what Jennifer said, and could not stop thinking about her top-secret job. For hours he attempted to process everything and took note to how she did manage to sidestep meeting in person once again. Brian thought about how much of a relief it was that Jennifer understood his chaotic schedule, odd work hours, and weekends, because she does it too. He thought, is she possibly one of his competitors and they have met already? Is she someone's wife!?!? Maybe she is a private investigator, FBI agent, a police officer (a girl in uniform… kinky…) he can already hear himself saying, "*Oh please arrest me!*" he probably does have a parking ticket she could probably help him with. (Wink) Or maybe she is a plumber and she is embarrassed, or works for the IRS, or her deceased grandmother is super wealthy and she is the recipient of a huge amount of money and she handles the family business, or maybe she is a sugar mama? He laid there and fanaticized about driving the Ferrari or the Bentley. He thought about her frequent trips and maybe they are on a private jet or maybe she has a yacht, he thought about how good of a pilot or a skipper he could be, shoot he would even go for being a stewardess—she did mention she is very well traveled. Maybe he finally hit the jackpot and he will have an easier life eating bonbons on the couch, lol!

For the next couple of weeks their routines continued as usual, and Brian kept a scratch pad nearby to take any notes he may catch as they conversed. Jennifer didn't bring up meeting in person, and he didn't press it either, Brian's plan was to be patient and wait for her to tell him her secret but Jennifer just kept on as always, being very bubbly, funny, and thoughtful, but there was absolutely no indication whatsoever about what she does for work or if she is buried in cash, or when they might meet in person. Brian is a VERY good reader of people in general from all walks of life, plus his gift to receive vibrations and energies to trigger his ESP into others' lives. Brian has received NOTHING from Jennifer, it is so unnatural for him, especially in this scenario, and the main and ONLY difference between everyone else and Jennifer is he has one on one human contact with everyone else, even strangers 50-75 yards away he can see what enlightens them or stalks them, but when it comes to Jennifer the closest contact he has had is electronic. He guesses this is his only kryptonite. Brian can literally feel the vibrations of people's moods and see their intentions, so Brian ALWAYS depressurizes and deflates bad things coming or tense situations by hugs and shaking hands or breaking the energy by engaging in conversation. Brian always says if more people made contact, the spirits and paranormal cannot attach because it is too complicated. Why? A possession is singular, when people touch, it is no longer mono-e-mono, and the stalkers move on. Think about that the next time you are buried in your phone.

The next time Brian and Jennifer were on one of their nightly conversation, he was in a trance going over his notes he had made over the last several weeks and all the data he had gathered about her profession, and trying to not be Captain Obvious, he heard her say, "Hey Brian are you there?" "Hello… Hey, are you there?" he replied, "*Yes…yes… I am sorry, I was just thinking*". Jennifer asked Brian what has been on his mind lately, because he seems to not be into their conversations, or what was going on with him? He went right to it and told her the only thing that's constantly on his mind is meeting her in person. She let him continue to speak… he explained he has thought about everything in depth, and if it is a deal breaker about them meeting in person, then it is a deal breaker, because he can't keep living like this. He professed how much he really values her, all that she is to him, how the last six months have been the best time of his life, but he joined the site to meet someone, and he can't think of anyone he would want to meet more than her.

Without a single hesitation Jennifer said, "Ok, babe, let's meet."

Brian was almost taken back by his request, and had this big overwhelming sense of guilt, but also butterflies the size of a commercial aircrafts fluttering around inside of his stomach. He almost couldn't speak! She offered to meet him in just two days, on Saturday night for dinner. From that moment they were making plans, neither had ulterior plans, they both promised to tell work they had prior obligations scheduled and would be unavailable on this night until midnight. Brian was ecstatic, it was finally going to happen, however he was nervous also. It was now officially past six months of carrying on in a steady committed relationship. Two people who fell in love for all the right reasons, whom have never met, but now they were going to finally meet in person. It became an instantaneous fun-filled conversation again between them. They laughed and laughed, teased each other again about the seriousness of meeting, they were back in their comfort zone, the honeymoon stage, and back to being deeply in love. They spent the rest of the night laughing until they both couldn't laugh anymore telling stories and comparing each other's past worst dates and compared them to their upcoming meet. Truth is nothing is going to stop the inevitable, it took longer than expected, but alas… they will meet, because they belong together.

CHAPTER NINE

SATURDAY HAD FINALLY ARRIVED! JENNIFER sent her regular good morning text at 6am, and said she felt like it was Thanksgiving and she needed to be up that early to get the turkey started. Brian never slept a wink; he was up all night for this much anticipated day. They coordinated everything and combed through every detail over the last two days, so they had their to do lists, one of which was NOT to talk all day, and only one hour prior to the big event. Brian was enthralled to finally meet the woman of his dreams. Jennifer was nervous, but very hopeful. This woman had every bit of Brian's attention, and his dreams felt like they were finally coming true. Jennifer had her day planned to do her lady things like a pedicure and manicure, eyebrows done, and several hours set aside to get ready. Jennifer did break the rules and needed Brian's opinion which matching panties and bra she was going to wear, because she always wore matching ones all from Victoria Secrets. Brian replied lace and minimal, and Jennifer's response was how about none? After her break of silence, they continued to remain playful and naughty throughout the day, the two of them always have so much fun!

When it became time to head out for the evening, they coached each other all the way to the parking lot of the restaurant they planned to eat at. They had planned to park at opposite sides of the parking lot, except someone screwed up because they ended up parking right next to each other. They marked that up to jinx because they often did all the same things the other did. It was the moment of truth, they hung up their phones, Brian's heart was pounding, and Jennifer's mouth was dry, and her hands were cold and sweaty. They were both about to meet their life partners and best friends all in one, and who they will spend the rest of their lives with. In synchronization, they got out of their cars at the same time and set eyes on each other for the first time ever in the flesh. They were both EXACTLY who they said they were, the moment was epic! They came face to face and both busted out laughed hysterically and gave each other a big hug. They were both still extremely nervous, so they walked side by side into the restaurant, they were seated for their reservation, and their conversations picked right up again from where they hung up just a few minutes ago. Everything was perfect, and everything that transpired between them for the last 6 months was now all here in front of the two of them. They enjoyed a full meal with appetizers, entrees, and desserts feeding each other, teasing one another, the evening followed their pre-determined schedule, Brian received his first intuition that Jennifer is extremely passionate, very detailed, expressive, and never saw any stalkers around her, however it may be because the two of them were touching each other's hands reached across the table throughout the night. What Jennifer did in her profession didn't matter at this point, because Brian was very admired to see how personable she was, and therefore is very connected with her clients which is why she is an expert at whatever it is she does. Brian was able to receive a message she felt many rewards from her work, she feels appreciated, and the responses are very enduring, and heartfelt for many years. The only questionable message he felt is she is guarded, and very protective. Brian wasn't focused on the energies he could see and feel that were overly expressed and loud, time will tell, he was too busy enjoying the time together.

The check had been sitting on the edge of the table for quite some time, when Brian reached for it, Jennifer suggested they pay equally their part of the check. Jennifer just got another point in Brian's book, however he insisted he cover the entire bill, and told her it was his wish to pay the bill to retain the image of the perfect gentleman. Within seconds of placing his credit card in the check holder, the server came by and grabbed it swiftly, clearly irritated they made her wait. Jennifer looked down at her watch, busted out laughing again, and said they had been at the restaurant for 5 hours. Brian responded "*5 HOURS!!!*" they got up to view all the chairs were up on the tables, all the other guests had left, and the two of them closed the establishment. The time had passed so quickly. When their check returned, Jennifer insisted on leaving a cash tip for the server, her treat. Could this woman be any more perfect? Jennifer left a crisp one-hundred-dollar bill in the check holder, and Brian paid the bill. They both approached the server, and thanked her graciously for her service, her patience, and the wonderful service. As Jennifer and Brian left the building, he walked her to the driver's side of her vehicle, he could feel the tension all the way in the back of his throat the two of them were going to be sharing their first kiss. Jennifer opened her car door, and they continued talking standing in the opening of the door. Brian was waiting for her look to say without words "kiss me". Brian leaned in trembling to kiss her, and she turned her head and hugged him instead. Brian followed her lead and went on ahead for a solid good hug. He could feel his heart pounding in his chest and could feel hers pounding right back. After a good long hug with some gentle back body rubs, he came back out for the kiss and Jennifer grabbed Brian's hand and shook it with a pushing away from her motion. She said briskly with her eyes the size of saucers "Goodnight, Brian, I look forward to seeing you again soon," pushing him back far enough she jumped in her car, locked the car doors, started it, and backed out swiftly almost running over both of his feet! She then slammed it into forward drive and sped out of the parking lot stopping for nothing. Brian watched her car speed away, slamming the front end of the car in the dip of the driveway, and heard the roar of her vehicle speeding away.

Brian was in utter disbelief of what just happened, he just stood there for a couple of minutes processing everything in lightspeed, looked down at his feet to see black tire marks across the tips of his shoes. He thought… well at least it was just over the roomy spot of the tip of his shoes, and thought to himself again, what just happened? A six-month romance of meeting the woman of his dreams to feeling like he just had dinner with his sister? Gosh, he hoped nobody saw that! Brian took the walk of shame over to his own vehicle, got in, sat there for a moment, thinking to himself, *Did that just really happen?* He reached into his glovebox, and there was still a pack of smokes in there from who knows how long ago, sometime in the last year, and shook one out and lit it. He took a long and slow big drag, inhaled, exhaled, and just then his phone began to ring. He looked at it, and it was her calling. He just let it ring on over to voicemail while he sat there smoking the cigarette inhaling and exhaling until the cherry on the end was two to three inches long and flicked it out the window. Jennifer kept calling and hanging up, she'd let it ring until it went to voicemail and hang up and call again. He finally clicked answer after the eighth or ninth time, but he didn't say anything. Jennifer said very expressively, "Hi babe, thanks for the amazing night, are you happy now that we met?" He was still silent, and simply hung up and turned his phone off all together. Brian was just stuck in a haze and could feel the buzz from not smoking for several months kind of blurring his eyesight, he was completely mortified. What just happened? He didn't even know what to think, so he just started the car and drove home in silence.

When he arrived home, he walked inside and was picking himself apart for being played for a fool, or was it "blue eyes" stalking him again? His heart had never been fuller in as long as he could remember, and now just thirty minutes ago it is squashed because he wanted to meet the girl? Was this her nasty game and punishment? When he finally turned his phone back on, before it even finished booting up it started ringing again, and Jennifer's name and photo showed across the screen. Brian went ahead and answered it, and she was talking so fast asking him where he was, she was deathly worried something happened to him on his way home, and Brian just remained silent letting her motor mouth run full blast talking about the whole night, how much fun it was, and our future dates, until Brian interrupted her and said, "*What was tonight?*"

Jennifer paused and said she didn't understand his question.

He said, "*I am sorry, I was under the impression for the last two days leading up to tonight, all the hype, all the planning, tonight was the night we would tie the knot and open our futures into the next phase of our relationship to seal our commitments with a kiss, just as we planned it out. Why didn't you kiss me?*"

Without even skipping a beat, she replied, "I don't kiss on the first date."

Brian was not only floored, but COMPLETELY puzzled, but he kept his calm, he knew he still wanted this woman for the long haul and decided to play along. He REALLY wanted to blast her, but he held his tongue, paused for a few seconds, played coy and said, "*Oh... ok... No biggie. I had a completely different understanding of what tonight was, I was just following the plan, so does that come on the second date?*"

Jennifer laughed hysterically and said, "Well if you are wondering, I don't f★ck on the third date either." She laughed even harder than she did at the beginning of her statement.

He thought to himself, *Wow, he had never even heard Jennifer say crap in the last six months, and she went straight for an f-bomb?*

She continued before he said anything at all. "I am not a piece of meat, Brian, like one of your other sluts. I am a respectable woman."

Again, he thought to himself, Whoa, wow… That also came out of left field too, he wasn't expecting that either. So he said back to her, *"Jennifer, I was only asking because I really like you and we have been talking and carrying on for many months in a loving-couple way as if we are in a full-blown relationship. Tonight seemed like it was the next step to our evolving romance."*

Before he could complete his sentence, Jennifer interjected again. "What, were you anticipating or wondering if you were going to be able to f★ck my brains out tonight? Did you plan to get me liquored up and take me home and have your way with me?"

He waited for her to take a breath and asked if she was talking or was he? She stopped her rant and told him to go ahead and talk. When he started, she jumped in a third time and said, "Sorry, I told you we should not have met."

He continued and said, *"Jennifer, I wasn't thinking about sex at all yet. I am happy we met, and—"*

She interrupted again. "I know about men. if I would have allowed you to kiss me it would not have stopped there. I don't like to be groped or forced." Laughing out loud, she continued, "I am a human being too, and I have a very strong appetite for sex, and fluid exchange. I have sex toys, I am not innocent. Do you know what BOB is, Brian?"

"Huh? What are you talking about?"

"BOB. All girls have a friend named BOB. Do you know what that is?"

"No, but I bet you are going to tell me."

Jennifer laughed hysterically again. "BOB is a battery-operated-boyfriend. I have had to have several BOBs for a long time because it has been so long since I have had the real thing. Why did YOU have to spoil everything and not just like me for me?"

Brian was completely caught off guard and with these continued attacks he decided to shift gears a bit. He said, *"Whoa, slow down, Jennifer. All I ultimately wanted to know is when I would get my first kiss, but you've gone on a complete tantrum about BOBs, which I have never even heard of before, sex toys, the real thing, and a strong appetite for sex. Hell, you are exactly my kind of girl!"* Brian continued; *"For six months I have completely followed your lead and your comfort zone, I have been patient, kind, understanding, and a complete gentleman. I took you out on our first date and only wanted a kiss goodnight, and you went to nymphomaniac sex-o-maniac in less than an hour after our date. I CAN'T wait for our next date!"*

Jennifer was completely silent on the other end of the phone for about the longest five minutes of his entire life, before piping up. "Brian…I…you know…ummm…I…uh…" and started laughing hysterically again. "I better go to bed. Can we talk tomorrow?" I have…um…a… I have a headache, I gotta go, BYE!"

CHAPTER TEN

THE NEXT MORNING, SUNDAY, BRIGHT and early, about 8am, Jennifer texted Brian to see if he was awake yet. He didn't immediately respond, he waited her out for a good couple of hours, responding back when he was good and ready with "Good Morning".

Jennifer responded right back, saying she knew he was awake for a couple of hours, she apologized for what transpired the night before and wanted to talk about plans for the second date. Of course, he wanted to see her again, so he asked her what she had in mind? Jennifer said she wanted to see him tonight, she reminded him typically Sundays are her get ready for the work week day, so she didn't want to meet up anywhere, she wanted him to come over to her house and show him her pride and joy being all her sports collections of her favorite team. She said she has a swimming pool and a hot tub and asked him to bring his swim wear, unless he preferred to go commando. Jennifer said she always swims naked, and wanted him to know clothing is optional, and to know there was no expectations. (Clearly she is throwing out some hints, don't you think?) Jennifer said anytime he wanted to come over to spend time with her it was an open invitation, but if he wanted a time, 6pm would be prime, because all of her Sunday duties would be done, and the whole evening would be theirs to spend together. Jennifer reminded Brian about how much she likes to cook, and would like to show him how great of a cook she is. Jennifer said for him to come hungry, and she already has some beer and wine and other beverages.

Jennifer continued to plan out the evening saying after the grand tour of her house, they can sit and talk, swim, watch a movie, and just have a nice evening together and if he was ok with that? Jennifer really seemed to pull a complete 180 from the night before, and as much as he liked her, his forgiveness was quick, and was really looking forward to the evening together. Jennifer also reminded Brian she has two cats, they are her children, and if he has any objections to them it is a deal breaker because she is not getting rid of her cats. Brian laughed and reminded her he also has a cat and a dog, so all animals are fine with the exception snakes. Jennifer laughed and said, "Oh yeah, we already had this discussion". She said she was just nervous, becomes forgetful when she is nervous, and she doesn't have many visitors, but enjoys being a host.

Brian asked her what he could bring? He reminded her his mother always says never to go empty-handed, so just say what it is he could bring and he would certainly pick it up on the way as well as call her on the way to ask if she needed any last ingredients or supplies. Brian was excited to spend the evening with Jennifer and expressed how excited he was to spend the evening with her. Jennifer told Brian the only other thing he could bring besides his handsome self, optional swim trunks his gleaming personality, he could bring a box of condoms. She said, "I am sorry I was a jerk to you last night, I hope I can regain your trust and confidence in me and we just have an enjoyable, romantic evening together. I am not promising or offering anything, but if the evening possibly goes in that direction, I am on the pill to regulate my menstrual cycles, so there is no way I can get pregnant, so we are safe". Brian said he would see her at 6pm and hung up. Brian sat in his family room processing what just occurred, he was excited, but also shocked, but maybe she has finally arrived to what the two of them have been working towards for many months. Was she bluffing him or being serious? He thought about standing her up, but the rule he lives by is No Risk, No Reward, so he decided to go for it and see what happens.

Men always play out the scenes in our minds, we love risk because we love the rewards, we think of plans what to do if something goes wrong, and how to plan accordingly of how it will go. Brian was cultivating if it will it be romance and love, or hot sweaty steamy gyrating crazy sex plus an all-night affair? She did say not to worry about pregnancy, but the golden rule is never believe that mumbo jumbo and always be prepared, not to mention avoiding STD's like the gift that keeps on giving (herpes). Bringing out the condoms can also send a lasting message there is a trust issue, or the guy is a gigolo, but sex is overrated and underrated. Brian for the first time realized he was intimidated by the scenario, and he does love her without having sex as the center of their ongoing love affair. Besides WHO DOES carry on with someone for months and months, says "I love you" daily, several times a day, with no physical action? This may just be the one he has spent his whole life waiting for, dreaming of, all his life. She is beautiful, she is cool, funny, has her own house, own money… She is EXACTLY what he configured, and it is all right here in the palm of his hands! She IS "THE ONE"!!

The day just crept by. Every time Brian looked at the clock only five or ten minutes passed. Brian was excited! He set his alarm for two hours before he needed to get ready for the night, he had waited his whole life for. When the alarm finally toned it was time, he shaved his face twice, going the normal way of down, and then again the opposite way to make sure he was Mr. Smooth Face. He took a long hot shower, dressed relaxed but still well, the right amount of cologne, and waited for the precise time to text her one last time to let her know he was on his way and get her address. She lived only 35 minutes away, which met another of his search criteria on the dating site. Everything was set, he did stop to grab a 3-pack of condoms on the way and headed to dreamland to see his queen!

CHAPTER ELEVEN

ONCE HE EXITED THE HIGHWAY, he drove down a beautiful road lined with trees, and then pulled into a very elegant neighborhood with huge houses lining both sides of the street, the houses in the neighborhood dwarfed his cozy bachelor pad. As he crept down the street having to look hard for each and every house number, he also went over about 5 of those huge annoying speed bumps, which clearly the HOA wants to keep the street traffic down to a slow speed to keep the noise down. Down near the end of the street stood a huge gray and white two-story house beautifully landscaped and a little fountain in the front yard. He pulled into a driveway with a very nice three-car garage, this was her house? Check that one off the list: "Big House." and he already has a place for his vehicle, and she has RV parking, so this would be "their" house? Brian went ahead and parked and just looked around for a moment taking it all in. He shut the car off, exited the vehicle, stretched, and continued looking around at the neighboring homes… this was way more than he had imagined, and he was beginning to get a sense of a life of settling down. He reached back into the car and grabbed his shaving lotion, put some in his hands, and applied it to his face to assure he would be greeting her smelling his best. He closed the door, locked it, and walked toward her front door. Before he had a chance to knock or ring the bell, she opened the door to greet him with a big smile on her face and said, "Welcome to my humble home." When she opened the door to allow him to walk in, the first thing he smelled was a honeysuckle fragrance, looking forward he could see a sitting room, a large curved staircase, vaulted ceilings, and quickly to the right two steps into the doorway stood the tallest, completely decorated Christmas tree. It was something out of a St. Nick's store with all the lights on, spinning ornaments, a train, and probably the nicest tree he had ever seen. He also noticed all around the windows surrounding the tree were spray-on snowflakes and other hanging ones around it also. It was odd considering it is mid-July and Christmas was seven months ago.

The rest of the house was also decorated very nicely, no other signs of Christmas anywhere else, or other holidays, but her home was very filled with arts and crafts. Her home was a spitting image of Jennifer as far as passionate, creative, detailed, with something just about everywhere he looked. Even the steps leading upstairs had positive affirmation plaques siting on opposing sides of each stair going up. The plaques read things like, "The best revenge is massive success," "A goal without a plan is just a wish," "It's not how big the house is, it is how happy the home is"—she also had four different cat condos sitting in different spots, very nice furniture, and clearly her showcase of her favorite sports team memorabilia everywhere he looked. She had several framed signed jerseys, signed helmets some sitting out, and other in cases, balls, cleated shoes tied and hanging on nails, and one of those life-size players on the wall. Jennifer was dressed in a short, body molded attractive white sundress decorated with sunflowers. She was so hot, and Brian was enamored by everything going on and how she looked, so when he turned to her for eye contact, Jennifer was standing in a front facing pose towards Brian about ten feet away, pulled up her dress in the front and said, "Look, no panties" giving Brian a full view of a landing strip cleanly shaven pubis and laughed hysterically. The two of them had not yet made any physical contact, she said she needed to go turn down the stove, and Brian headed back over to take a closer look at the Christmas tree.

Brian was examining all the different decorations on the tree, there were moving ornaments, some were snow globes, bubbling lights, some flashing lights, some steady lights, icicles, homemade ornaments, just about every kind he could think of and ones he had never seen before. He spoke loudly enough for her to hear him in the other room asking, if she keeps the Christmas tree up year round? Jennifer like a good host walked in asking if he liked it as she was drying her hands with a towel. He complimented her on the creativity and the beautiful tree, and asked if there are other holiday decorations around the house for other times of the year? Jennifer first said of course, and said she shoots off fireworks every weekend giggling and said although she really enjoys all the different holidays throughout the year, she said there was something about the wiring or wattage associated with the tree or the electrical wiring in the house and it all seems to be surrounded around where the tree is. She said electricians have been out to look at things, but everything checks out normal, so all she can figure is the decorations must carry the correct amount of wattage or something because ONLY the tree keeps the rest of the house happy. She said, "I wish I could take it down, but whenever she unplugs the tree, the lights in the kitchen go off, her alarm keypad starts beeping, her TIVO loses all of her recorded shows, and it blows a bunch of the breakers."

Brian was completely confused, and explained that is not how electricity works Jennifer, it is when you overload a circuit it blows breakers, and Christmas lights run very minimal volts, wattage and amps, so the likelihood of it blowing various breakers around the house when you unplug it, no wonder the electricians can't troubleshoot it. *"What does it do when you plug it in?"* Jennifer was rolling her eyes and said, "I know, I know, I have heard this same spiel multiple times like I am a stupid hopeless woman" she threw her hands in the air and acted like a damsel in distress, and then sarcastically and dramatically explained in a very animated way how it is a huge fiasco to unplug the stupid tree, let everything go off, plug the tree back in, and then go all the way around the house back and forth in a certain combination to reset the breakers. She added she has to reset her house alarm so it doesn't beep until it is set up again, reset all the clocks in the house, she has to reset her DVR to record all of her favorite programs again, re-do the pool timer, so she just leaves the tree plugged in year-around instead. She said, "It is an eye catcher though and beautiful, right?" He smiled and said, *"Of course it is, but I still want to see this in action (ha)."* She walked in, around him, reached down and unplugged the Christmas tree. Within seconds, just as she described, the kitchen lights all went out, one light bulb in the kitchen actually popped, and the alarm key pad started beeping. She said, "SEE!!!" Brian was completely floored, he had never seen anything like this before!! He followed her lead as they plugged the tree back in, went outside and reset the breakers even though none of them were popped to his inspection, but they clicked them all to the off position and back to the on position, walked back inside and sure shit, the tree was back on, and so was everything else!! He helped her reset clocks, and he grabbed a chair to stand on to replace the blown light bulb in the kitchen track lighting. She thanked him for being a thoughtful man, and naturally they just both headed back into the front room to continue their conversation about the tree. Brian then heard a small child's voice, it said, "Oh my baby boys... Mama wuvs you soooooo much," as she darted out in front of him to pick up one of her two cats who were now laying under the Christmas tree. Brian swore to himself the voice he heard was NOT Jennifer's, he had never NEVER heard this voice in the entirety they had been together. Jennifer picked up a large tabby-colored cat holding him like a baby saying in the same child's voice, "baby boy, this is your new da-da, he wuvs you so much, not like Mommy wuvs you, but he will," then rubbed her face all over the cat's body, and then holding him in the air from under the cats front arms and asked Brian if he wanted to hold his first born son. In that same moment Brian watched another cat still under the tree, a black and white tuxedo cat, with his front legs drag his back legs and body across the floor and all the way up the stairs. Brian felt some drool hit his hand from his mouth hanging open, and quickly asked her what is wrong with the other cat, does he always drag his body like that, or is he paralyzed? She put the tabby cat on the floor and explained the other cat has diabetes and that's a side effect, she said he isn't in pain or anything, but she must give him a shot every day to keep him alive and healthy. Curious, Brian asked if the tuxedo cat goes up the cat post like that? She laughed and asked Brian if he would like a demonstration? It was hard for him to say no, he had to see this! Jennifer ran up the stairs to get him which the cat's claws were seriously dug into the carpet as if he didn't want to be picked up or disturbed, but she released each of his nails encouraging the animal to show his trick. The same thing happened when she picked up the tuxedo cat in the same child's voice "My wittle boy, mama wuvs you sooooo much, she carried him down, put him on top of the five foot cat condo, and held him with one hand telling him to wait. Brian stood there in complete disbelief, as she took two steps back, and the cat literally tumbled down to the floor, and then drug his body across the floor and all the way back up to the top of the stairs again. Jennifer was laughing hard, and said, "Cheap entertainment huh?" She said she can't get enough of watching him do that, but he is such a loveable cat!

Brian was without words, he said to her "*Jennifer, you are definitely the most unique, person I have ever dated. Christmas trees in July that pop breakers, paralyzed cats, you have made the top-three list.*"

Jennifer laughed and asked which top-three list, because she belongs at the top of **Most Weird Girlfriends**, as she proudly claimed her award bowing and laughing as usual.

Jennifer took Brian by the hand into her living room, she walked him through each of her collection items, telling him a short story about each of them consisting of when she got them, what she had to do to get them… Some she bought online, some she stood in lines for hours, some were by luck of the draw, but each item was nicely in a shadow box or framed. She had pillows with her team's name all over her couch, she had blankets, slippers, framed ticket stubs, she showed him jackets, hats, gloves, socks, and even the toilet paper in one of the bathrooms had "most-hated opponent" on the paper for you to wipe your bum with she advised not to use, and the regular paper was on the side of the toilet. Jennifer was very proud and really enjoyed touring Brian through everything she had collected. Jennifer stopped and turned to Brian asking if he was ready for the grand finale.

He replied: "*Yes, of course, yes… I am very excited to learned all about you.*"

Jennifer led Brian through the house and into her kitchen where on the furthest west side of the room stood a gorgeous tall antique china cabinet. She was very excited to show him she also had a full set of dishes, plates, glasses cups, saucers, silverware, and cloth napkins of the same team on display all throughout her house. They stood side by side as she continued explaining everything was a separate purchased item, and how she was able to build the sets of players exactly to her liking taking several years to get it just right. Inside of the cabinet to the right in front of where Brian was standing were some very old turn of the century china, a crystal candy bowl, some other crystal items of which Brian is a connoisseur of antiques, and these were in pristine condition and very beautiful. Brian was observing the workmanship and the glistening of the sparkles as Jennifer continued talking about all her sport collection dishes. As Brian continued to glare at the precious china he smelled a faint, horrific odor filling his nostrils. The odor caused his nose to start to tickle like a sneeze was coming on, but he just scrunched his face to brush it off. Brian was staring at the antique dishes and actively listening to her full-on explanation of the players, their years, what year, their positions, their numbers, and asked Jennifer about the old china, how long she had it, and where did it come from? She quickly said it all belonged to her grandmother and kept talking about the team dishes. Brian suddenly smelled the odor again, but this time it was strong, and had a distinctive smell such as a mixture of rotten potatoes and spoiled meat. His nose started burning from the odor and itching badly, and felt static electricity charging up which he is very familiar with when it comes to old antiques. Brian can often feel the life of objects, their love, their admiration, the years the items have been well kept and passed along in generations. The static feeling is normal, an itchy nose is a presence attached to old objects, but this god-awful smell is new, and can't remember experiencing something like this around any kind of old antiques. The smell was so horrific, growing and fading in strength, and when it came on the strongest, he could almost taste it. This was very unusual, so he breathed into his hand and smelled it to make sure it wasn't his breath, he turned his nose upward and took a whiff, and it wasn't anything she was cooking, he pulled open the collar of his shirt to smell himself, and all he smelled was his cologne, it wasn't him. He interrupted Jennifer and asked if she smelled anything? She stopped in her descriptions, took a slow deep and long whiff, and said she didn't smell anything at all, and asked what it smelled like? He said, "*I am not sure, but something rank, maybe the garbage, or possibly something dead?*" With that vary statement Brian's injured leg started to ache badly, climbing in synchronization of his heartbeat. The pain kept climbing, the odor kept fading in and out, the itchy face, and a dry mouth, he felt there was a presence in the room, but didn't mention anything to her thinking it might scare her, and just said he was feeling thirsty. Jennifer said, "Well if you just wanted me to stop talking about my pride and joy instead of acting like you were interested, and backing out saying you are thirsty, just tell me next time and I will stop!" Brian told her he was very interested in everything she had to say, but his leg was sore from standing a lot, and he was getting parched. She obliged and said, "Sure honey, no biggy" and grabbed his hand and walked him over to the couch to sit down. She reached down and loosened his shoestrings, took off his shoes, put a pillow under his feet, and said she would fetch them something to drink. As she walked away into the kitchen and they were away from the china hutch, all the symptoms faded away almost completely and his leg pain was at least tolerable at this point. Brian continued to process the situation, he didn't see anything, but felt perhaps an entity, but then again maybe the trash was just outside and just a breeze carried the odor in.

After about 10 minutes of sipping water and resting, Jennifer grabbed Brian's hand again tugging him to get up explaining she doesn't get many visitors, at least ones who stay a while. She was clearly loving every minute they were sharing and wanted to continue the tour. She took him to the patio door, led him outside and showed him the pool area, it was also very nicely decorated to resemble something you would see at a resort with palm trees, citrus trees, flowers, very trimmed and very green grass, lounging chairs, and plenty of pool gear to play in the water. Her pool even had a waterfall and sprayers shooting the water in the air. Then it was off to view the huge garage where the floor was epoxied, painted walls, and lined with storage cabinets, she paraded him through the kitchen and pointed out how the kitchen used to be, and all of the remodeling she had done, back through an arched hallway and back around to the Christmas tree room as she pointed upward to the vaulted ceilings and pointed out where she had a leak and the ceiling was stained from the water, and a very long piece of drywall tape was hanging down right over the top of the Christmas tree. Brian had not noticed the leaky spot before, and understood why she pointed it out, she was embarrassed by it, so she wanted to make sure he knew it was there and why. She said, "Are you ready to go upstairs?"

Jennifer lead Brian as they went up about five stairs to a small landing, and there laid the tuxedo cat who quickly drug himself down the five stairs and scurried out of site. They then headed upward for another 17 more stairs to a loft with a couple of chairs overlooking most of the first floor, there was a set of double doors leading somewhere else, and Jennifer pointed down the hallway to the right describing the first door on the right is a bathroom, the next door on the right is a closet, the open door at the end of the hallway is a bedroom, coming back this way the left, two other single doors are more bedrooms, and then they faced the double doors. Brian was thinking it was a game room and the door at the end of the hallway with the open door was the master bedroom. Jennifer then opened the two Dutch doors at the same time and said, "This is my room, the master, where I will be the master tonight and you Brian will be my slave," and gave her best Dracula laugh, followed by another one of her joking hysterical laughs! Brian thanked her for the amazing grand tour, complimented her on having a beautiful house, turned around to head back downstairs only to hear the child's voice again. This time it said, "Is hims going on another field trip?" Brian knew this time it was her, but asked for clarification what she was talking about? Jennifer described several days a week her cats go down the long hallway to the open door room and they meow and howl standing in the corner. Before Brian could respond, she continued in the child voice, "It's ok... I am watching...

go on... go on, it's ok my sweet prince... mommy left the door open for you... mommy is watching." As she waived the large tabby cat to walk down the hallway with its tail straight up in the air hugging the wall with his body. She encouraged the cat, and Brian stood there with his mouth hanging open again as they watched the animal go in the room, sit down, and start meowing and howling. Jennifer laughed and laughed again pointing to how hysterical and cheap the entertainment is to watch her cat act stupid meowing at a blank wall, and the tumbling tuxedo cat. Brian was at a loss for words...

CHAPTER TWELVE

JENNIFER GRABBED BRIAN'S HAND TO lead him into her bedroom which he could feel his leg start pinging with pain again, his face started to tickle, and the odor from downstairs was present again. Brian KNEW at this point something else was there besides the two of them, and the cats. He turned to her, grabbed both of her hands, and said, "*Jennifer, I need to ask you a question?*"

Jennifer turned responding quickly "Sure."

Brian said, "*Have you ever had your house cleansed before?*" Jennifer angrily jerked away and angrily said, "What are you implying, that my house is DIRTY!?!?" She shouted, "YOU don't f*cking know ME, and the first time you come to my house, I am a perfect host, I give you the grand tour, which NOBODY gets, and you insult me!?"

Brian said, "*Jennifer, of course not, your house is beautiful, very clean, very tidy, and I am honored to be here. I don't think you understand what I am asking.*"

Jennifer replied, "Then what the f*ck do you mean, has my house ever been cleansed? I work very hard to keep this house very cleansed, thank you very much!"

Brian explained. *It is a different kind of cleaning, it is an energy purification. When we all go out into the world day after day, we pick up bad and negative energies and bring them back into our homes. Those spirits collect day after day setting up shop right inside of homes. A cleansing is done periodically throughout the year, sometimes monthly, to bless your home granting passage of the bad spirits to leave and keep your house open to supporting positive energies to remain keeping your space healthy".* Jennifer busted out laughing hysterically with tears pouring down her face she was laughing so hard. She said, "Brian, I don't believe in anything like that because I work around enough dead people, if there is a spirit at all of any kind they are definitely not in dead people!"

Brain paused…started to speak…paused again, and said, "*Whoa… Wait… Are you by chance a mortician?*"

Jennifer turned almost white with a blank look on her face and became very defensive. She threw her hands up and pointed at him, saying, "This is all your fault, you are the one who wanted to meet, so this is where I get dumped, right? What difference does it make what I do?"

Brian explained to Jennifer calmly assuring her it doesn't matter what she does for a living, but he has a very strong sixth sense which is connected through the chronic pain he lives with in his badly disfigured and painful bad leg. He explained it is his pain which acts like a dinner bell attracting the unruly, destructive, negative, mean, and evil spirits by default because they are always around to investigate his chronic pain. He explained to her while he has been in her home he had experienced some very odd and unusual circumstances. He asked her "*Doesn't the fact you being a mortician and me with a sixth sense have an unusual rhyme to it?*"

Jennifer was just waiting for the moment for her to talk again, and instead started screaming loudly "Yes… I am a mortician, but I am very good at what I do, and I am NOT going to change my profession for you or anyone else! I change lives, Brian, I work on the really hard cases of people who commit suicide, lots of children, old people, mutilated bodies, and people of the very wealthy, who, when they want a really nice job, or make people who come from horrific circumstances look really good, they all come to me. If this is going to create a problem, you can just leave right now."

Brian suggested they just take a breath and relax for a few and start over. Brian was still feeling the pain in his leg, smelling the odor, and the itchy face, but Jennifer insisted she was fine, and could continue talking right now. Brian obliged her request and she went on to tell him she was born to be a mortician, explaining it takes a very special person in a certain kind of way to do what she does. She explained since she was a young girl, she knew it was her calling, and her vocation. Brian remained silent other than telling her to continue, he was listening... Jennifer gave a rather ugly face almost as if she was mocking him for not losing his cool and changed her mood again. She sat down on the end of the bed detailing how when people finally know what she does for work, people lose all of their interest in her, some people give the mortified disgusted look and just walk away, and she said MANY great conversations between her and others suddenly turn to asking her to show them dead bodies. With a frustrated jerking motion, she yelled looking toward the ceiling and said, "Why am I no longer interesting for just being ME!?!?"

She continued explaining all conversations turn into this horrific ideology she is this made up Hollywood character of an undertaker of some horror flick or some made up bullshit story comparing her many times to a dark eerie being when this is just her profession and she takes pride in what she does, just like other people do in their professions. She explained the living is the darkness of this world and the deceased, her clients are her true friends! Jennifer said she is who gives her friends a defense and a voice, because she can relate to being bullied, picked on, teased, and it takes her back to her memories as a youth. She said when new friends arrive, and she views the body she immediately is side by side in unison with the greater portion of her clients who arrive from self-inflicted suicides. She said, "the most rewarding part of her time with her clients is they are in fact really good listeners." She said, "Brian, they are so peaceful, they agree with everything I say, they are non-judgmental, there is no time limit, and while we work together happily to get them ready to leave this disgusting, judgmental, sad, harsh and meaningless world, I am always leaving for the day feeling appreciated." She said every day she gets back to work she is welcomed; her friends are smiling and greet her when she returns to continue the conversation again where they left off. Brian remained listening without changing his demeanor and Jennifer turned up the conversation a bit by saying "Yes, I take an extremely passionate and caring approach at orchestrating a very meaningful final farewell to the families who never stood by them, their so called friends who ignored my clients calls for help, and especially to their bullies to never forget their damages they caused my beautiful friends." Jennifer said she enjoys the crying, the stress, the pain, the locked faces in loss or the concern of the onlookers who should have done something to prevent this situation, she said it really gives her a sense of accomplishment, and she really did her job well.

CHAPTER THIRTEEN

JENNIFER REACHED OUT TO BRIAN grabbing his hand to sit down on the bed next to her, she said passionately "Brian, I really, really enjoy watching people in loss and sorrow. The number or tears, shrills, moans, and screams I can create is my bravo, my applause, and very rewarding meaning I delivered a seamless performance and my friend received their final satisfaction they wanted, and I assisted them fulfilling their final wish." Jennifer explained suicide is a cry for help so strongly committed someone is willing to die for it. Jennifer said she has done so many of these she sides with the deceased to get their message across. She said again her profession is very rewarding because she is very familiar with the amount of teasing, bullying, depression, lonely confinement, having her hair pulled, picked at, being called ugly, chubby, clumsy, or dorky and even in her adult life attacked again for her profession, this is her bittersweet revenge."

When Jennifer released Brian's hands to continue talking, instantly Brian saw shadowy profiles surrounding her in sort of a huddle like football players do making plays on a field. His leg was pounding, his nose full of tickling, his sixth sense depicted four spirits in the room with them. Brian reached over and held her hand again and the images vanished immediately, and the symptoms lightened up. Jennifer continued talking about her work, she sees it as kind of like a rehabilitation center. She gets these people from all walks of life, most of them interrupted with their final message to the world and they instantly become friends because they share the same feelings. She said, "Brian, do you know what it is like to tell a complete stranger your deepest feelings and they don't judge you, and they lay there peacefully listening?" She said she can dress them up however she wants, she is so talented they play dress up together, she can create whatever expressions she wants, put them in whatever pose she wants, and it is customary they always share at least one or two meals together. She said every day ends with her feeling fully appreciated, all her worries, concerns, decisions, just everything has been lifted off her chest with zero judgements, she feels totally fulfilled, loved and admired. She described every new friend and clients she meets she gets to learn all their points they connect on by first meeting the families and learning how her client suddenly has a very appreciated valued interest to the family. She described the guilt, the faultlessness, the twisted families are all the same who until before their death, the person was meaningless. Suddenly now they have extreme value and the family wants the deceased to have the very best outing from the living world. The families want certain outfits, a certain look, prize possessions inside of the caskets, to the point she is she is intoxicated with exactly how she is going to drive the spike in to fulfill her new friend's final wishes. It is very clear to him Jennifer is extremely passionate about her career, but excessively to the point it is every part of her wellbeing

Jennifer jumped off the bed and excitedly said, "Brian, there is a secret about all of what I do I have never admitted to anyone. You know what it is? "Can you keep a secret and promise not to judge me, and not ever tell anyone"?

Brian replied, "*I haven't so far, lay it on me, what do ya got?*"

Jennifer said, "I sometimes get clients who are John Doe's, with no next of kin, or clients who their next of kin are only paying for their services because they have too, so I have turned those into rewards for me also, because they don't get any services, it is just get them ready and they go right into Potters Field" (Potters Field is a place of burial of the unknown or indigent people).

Brian just sat their listening, and said, "*ok?*"

She said, for those people she dresses them up and puts on their makeup to resemble her bullies from throughout her life. She throws trinkets of her past into the box, and buries her bullies, her hardships, her problems right along with the deceased jerk. Jennifer says she can always drive down memory lane if she needs too, and can visit her past when she wants too, but otherwise her past is buried forever, just like her child psychiatrist her parents MADE her go too said she needed to learn how to bury her problems, laughing out loud about it.

Jennifer thought up somethings else and said, "Brian, do you know I even embalmed and prepared my own grandmother?" He didn't have any physical contact with her at the time of the announcement, but he immediately smelled that same odor again and this time it was gagging strong and his leg pain went to level nine buzzing like a freshly smacked tuning fork. She looked at him and said, "OMG, stop it, you are fine", as he asked to go back downstairs. To him it was like she never even heard him, so Brian reached over again to touch her in attempt to stop the entity, which again, it lessened instantly to a tolerable level so he could keep listening.

She continued explaining, "Brian, embalming my grandmother is really where everything changed for me in my career". She described how she grew up and stayed in the small town again like she did in their first month together. She said her family settled there back in the 1800's and they've all remained for many generations in a circumference as far as fifty miles away, and nothing further. Small town mentality is exactly what you hear and read about... Everybody knows everybody, and everybody knows everybody's business. Just the same when someone dies, everyone knows about this too, and everyone knew she was the undertaker. Through all the years of being a mortician in a small town the money was terrible because of the infrequency and when someone died it was the talk of the town how bad the person looked. She said, "Brian, I was getting it from both ends all the time". Her grandmother always supported her 100%, g'ma was always there to look after her, and supported her through all her life. Jennifer described the people in that small town, instead of honoring the someone who died, they cackled, joked, and poked just like they did to her for her entire life! She said it was her utmost honor to prepare her grandmother for her final rest, and although she misses her every day and every moment to this day, it was the blessing in disguise that launched her career.

Jennifer described again in immense detail how she took her time giving her grandmother her very best talents. She polished her nails, cut her hair, permed it, put on her makeup, dressed her in her finest Sunday dress and her favorite hat. She said during the several days they had together, she was able to talk to her g'ma and reminisce, and it was the best last few days of her life with her very special g'ma. At the funeral, the entire town and everyone in the 50 miles around us came. People came from other states, other churches, and when the viewing came Jennifer stood at the head of the casket next to her g'ma in honor of her, and the attendees cried out loud, some fainted, hundreds of people placed items in her casket, and it took three long days to allow everyone time with my g'ma. Jennifer said it was the single proudest moment of her entire life.

Jennifer said so many of the people who teased her for years, pranked her, set her up to be the butt of all their jokes, did a 180 and praised her for such a magnificent well done job. Her talents changed an entire population of people from miles around from bad to very respected, and it was all because of her passionate talent. Jennifer said from that day going forward she knew her mission in life was to send the message of the deceased to change people forever. She proudly states she knows she has made a loud statement on the lives and hearts of all people by the response of her clients and the honor she receives at the job she values most.

Jennifer jumped up again and said, "I want to show you something, I think this explains me completely and fully to a T." She went over to a big chest in her room, opened it, talking about something she had inside she loves. She was talking out loud about a special shirt she wears every day as an undergarment like Superman wears his S, she said she bought them in bulk, she could only get fifty of them, so she bought them in every color she could get. She grabbed 2 items from the chest, walked back across the room into her bathroom, closed the door, and Brian could hear her rustling around in there. She walked out of the bathroom backwards wearing pajama bottom baggy pants and did a jump spin move and with a silly face, she pointed at her shirt with both pointer fingers and read off what the shirt said. It said, "I put the FUN in FUNERAL," Jennifer was laughing hysterically like always. She then said, "Brian, you ARE absolutely the coolest, greatest, amazing man I have ever met!" She said, "You never ran from me, interrupted me, treated me like a lady, didn't judge, and I proudly am going to give you what you have waited six long months to get starting right NOW!!!

Jennifer ran towards Brian still sitting on the bed, and dived football tackled him the rest of the way onto the bed. She was completely on top of him with her left hand fully and forcefully grabbing his junk in his crotch, her right hand was pinning down his hands over the top of his head while she was heavily breathing in his mouth, clanking her teeth against his shoving her tongue into his mouth, while she was hot and heavy all over him. Brian reached down to unbuckle his belt and undo his jeans, but before he got to his hip, he felt a bunch of small hard pieces all over the bed. As she was going crazy for him, all he did was swish his hand around seeing how and where the pieces were coming from and stopped her to say there is gravel or something all over the bed. Jennifer said, "it is from the cats, they sleep in my bed, and it is just a little bit of cat litter they don't always get off their feet.

Brian thought throughout all the commotion going on "*is the raunchy stench he keeps smelling actually a combination of cat piss and cat shit, and it is now in the same bed and I am rolling all over in it?*" He could hardly breathe between the stank, her in his mouth, her on top, and forcibly all over him, so he went for HER crotch, and as soon as he did that, she stopped all of her action, and curled up next to him spooning on their right sides and she said in a very a sweet soft voice "can you just hold me for a while... it has been a very long time since she had simply just been held, and even longer from a man." As they laid there spooning, Brian was pondering quietly weighing everything in his mind. He had put in all this time, effort, and commitment into this woman, and NEVER imagined in his wildest dreams something like this would find its way to him through the valleys and streams of the pained paranormal. Was she talking and carrying on with him for all these months like she did with the deceased only because they hadn't met? Just as he finished that thought he felt Jennifer nudge in deeper against him and pulled his arms around her and told him to kiss her neck. He did as she wished, and started running his tongue around a bit, and gently sucked, and she said, "don't lick me like a dog, I said kiss, nothing else". He just laid his head back down on the pillow holding her. Brian's leg was pounding in pain, but he was not going to let it win this time, he tried his best to hold the position anticipating more would follow before long. Ten minutes, twenty minutes, thirty minutes, and she wasn't moving, but he could start to see shadows moving in, but in no repetitive motions, but in a fashion to inspect Jennifer and Brian. He said to her, "*Jennifer, you know you have spirits here in your house who don't like sharing you, don't you?*" Jennifer rolled over, facing him with a concerned look on her face. She asked who? Brian said, "*I can sense 4 at the moment, two are young children, another is a teenager, and the last is a woman, possibly older, but I am not completely certain yet.*" Jennifer kept the same look on her face and said, "Well I guess they are in for a show tonight, but just keep holding me, everything will be ok, I am about ready." He wondered what she was about ready for since up to this point everything from the moment they met has been completely unpredictable. Maybe the food cooking downstairs was about finished, maybe she was finishing up an innocent siesta, or maybe hot sex was on the way… nonetheless he negotiated with himself he was already there, likely the worst was over, so he decided to see what comes next.

After about another ten minutes, Brian started to feel that same tickly feeling in his nostrils as it gradually covered most of his face, he could smell the rotten odor again over the honeysuckle house fragrance lurking in. What was significantly different this time is he was in complete contact with her, and his leg pain was pinpointed right at the original break zone. This was very unusual to him, but more importantly the odor absolutely was not him, the bed, the house, and Jennifer smelled like a hint of vanilla. Brian asked her if she smelled anything unusual. She told him to stop, and just lay with her, she said maybe one of the cats just went pee-pees or poo-poos and she is just used to it, because she doesn't smell anything at all. Brian was certain it WASN'T pee-pees or poo-poos and insisted it was something wrong like a backing up sewers or something. He asked her again if she really didn't smell anything at all?

Jennifer rolled back over to face him, and said, "FINE!!" Jennifer strongly pinned both of Brian arms back on the bed again and started forcing her face and mouth right into his, forcibly kissing him so hard he could feel her teeth raking against his like a washboard. She then stood on the bed whipped her pants off and took her fun in funeral shirt off baring her completely naked body to him and said, "Well, why aren't you naked yet?!?" Brian was just looking up in disbelief what just took place in the last thirty seconds and possibly wanting to look at her nakedness for the first time. Without a missed beat, she pounced right back down on top of him, grabbing for his jeans waist line pulling with force his tucked in shirt, then went for undoing his jeans wrestling trying to get his belt unbuckled. While Jennifer was insistently at work and Brian laying on his back trying to help where he could, suddenly the same horrific odor smacked him right in the face so dense and so strong it filled his nose and mouth with it he could taste it. Then he felt all the fingers of a hand go around his bad leg precisely at the most painful break spot, squeeze hard with immense strength jerking him down toward the end of the bed from beneath Jennifer about a foot. Brian sat right up letting out a scream, "*AGGGHHHH! GET OFF OF ME JENNIFER!!!!*" He pushed her off him with great force to get to his leg. When Brian took his next breath, he felt a full-sized big fat object the size of a marble, fly into his mouth hitting his top lip, the front of his teeth, then the back of his throat, and going all the way down his esophagus. Brian immediately started choking and gagging, and coughing trying to get it back up and made it somehow onto the floor near her bathroom door. He looked to find Jennifer, looked around again in complete horror where she was, and she had the 'FUN in Funeral' shirt back on sitting on the bed watching him flailing around on the floor. Brian then felt intensely ill, his leg in immense pain more then he can remember, his head was pounding with each pound into a severe migraine headache, his stomach started thrashing with severe stomach cramps, his skin felt like glass shards were coming through the surface, and his hands and feet were as cold as if they were in buckets of ice water. He felt convulsive pains throughout his torso as if he was going into full on and complete organ failure. Then his vision began to blur, it felt like his eyes were popping out of their sockets, and his tongue felt like it was ten times larger than normal size causing him unable to breathe. Brian pulled himself up to the bathroom sink, flipped on the bathroom light, and turned on the faucet. Before he splashed the water on his face, he looked into the mirror, and his skin was so white it had a bit of a greenish tint to it. He continued gasping for air to the point he began snorting. His insides were twisted up into knots, and he slid back down onto the cold tile floor laying in the fetal position shaking in fury.

Jennifer walked in standing over him screaming angrily. "You are so f*cking sarcastic and ridiculous, you are such a drama queen, is this how you treat all your sluts who don't whip their clothes off at your command and let you screw their brains out!?!?" While he gasped for air, he shouted back, "*Does it really f*cking look like I am faking it?*" She flung open the medicine cabinet grabbing each of the items throwing them at him in a great downward force, screaming "WHAT DO YOU NEED, SOME ASPIRIN, SOME COUGH SYRUP, HOW ABOUT SOME F*CKING MINT FLAVORED DENTAL FLOSS!?!? OH WAIT, MAYBE THIS WILL HELP, SOME MIDOL FOR PMS, YOU STUPID SON OF A BITCH, MAYBE SOME FACE WIPES, YOU ASSHOLE USING PRICK!!!" When she emptied everything, she gave a loud scream stomping out of the room and down the stairs yelling at someone named Donny. He could hear her downstairs in a full-on argument with someone as he laid on the floor trying to pull himself together. He was breathing heavily, sweating so much his clothes were drenched while he shook in immense pain. The odor was gone, the shadows were gone, and he could still hear Jennifer downstairs yelling different sentences in different voices. She'd say in a deep voice, "I told you not to meet him or bring him over here"; to her voice, "He is my friend, aren't I allowed to have friends?"; then the deeper voice again, "I say who is allowed and not allowed, and your broke the rules young lady." her voice, "You don't know me!"; then a moment of silence…then her voice again, "I don't know…. I don't KNOW when he is going to leave"; silence…followed by the deep voice, "GET OUT OF MY HOUSE!"; her voice, "No, he is my friend and he can stay as long as he wants"; deep voice, "You stupid bitch, you don't deserve any friends"; then the familiar child's voice, "Donny, it will be ok, he will be leaving soon."

Brian managed to get up and while still immensely sick, as quickly and as quietly as he could limp and damper his groans, he made his way to the bedroom door. Now at the top of the stairs he slowly eased down the staircase keeping watch for wherever she might be and praying not to be seen. As he made his way down the seventeen stairs to the lower landing Jennifer was over at the china hutch pleading Brian is just a friend… he has already left… and so on. She must have heard Brian trying to leave because she turned around, eye locked with Brian like a parent might catch a child spying. She had a very angry look of disgust on her face, she turned around and beelined right at Brian in such a manner like the same parent would be going to spank the spying child. Brian with all his inner strength made it to the front door before she could get to him and they met again face to face. They didn't say anything to each other, just glaring at each other, and Brian swears he saw the twinkle in her eye of something very evil. Brian reached to open the door, and she was right there holding it open for him to slowly limp out of the house. As soon as Brian was three to four steps outside, Jennifer slammed the door with such force, it opened again. He could hear her yell "GOD DAMN DOOR" and she slammed it again and he could hear her engage all the locks inside as a statement Brian was locked out and unable to come back in.

CHAPTER FOURTEEN

BRIAN LIMPED TO HIS CAR, got in, and sped out of there stopping for nothing all the way home. After a thirty-five minute drive away from her house, the pains and symptoms had not let up at all. Brian went into his house as quickly as he could, once inside he stripped off all of his clothing and hung his head in the toilet to gag, dry heave, and tried sticking his fingers down his throat attempting to throw up whatever it was that flew in his mouth, in hopes of feeling better immediately. Brian tried, and he tried, and he tried, and nothing came up at all. He hung over that toilet processing how he had already exceeded all the odds suffering for almost twenty years in chronic pain, surged ahead of all the doctors multiple misdiagnosis and all of their surgeries, accomplished so many things, stitched up, stapled up, sleepless nights, bleeding and in agonizing pain and this should be NOTHING compared to all he has accomplished. It was shameful in his mind as he wept like a newborn baby. With all the same symptoms he caught from her house, he laid naked on his bathroom floor for three days. His phone never rang, nobody came to check on him, he used the bath rug for a blanket and the toilet paper roll for a pillow.

He had never been sicker in all his life, and the leg pain was the most horrific he could ever remember. He thought back to the night of the pain he experienced when his leg was crushed by a motor in a head-on car crash, and this was WORSE! For those three days he felt he was steps from dying in his bathroom, and it would have been just fine with him. Anything to stop this pain and the spastics twists and turns of his torso, the blindness, the cold limbs, why won't it STOP!!!

On the morning of the fourth day, he woke not knowing the time of day, but everything had passed! He felt completely normal like he had never been sick at all, so he immediately looked down to his leg to examine it. His leg had the darkest and deepest blue, black, and greenish bruise he had ever seen. He carefully and closely examined his leg, and the bruising was exactly where he had broken his leg originally. Brian reached up into his bathroom drawer where he kept a sewing measuring tape because it is made of cloth to measure the width of the bruise and it measured just over seven inches wide, and it was all the way around his leg. The original break was about four inches above his ankle, so everything from the ankle joint, passed the break and upward was blackened and extremely painful. The bruise also had the appearance of a large hand had squeezed it, because the bruise lines were four stripes and a bit more on the top to resemble a thumb. It definitely was not like he had badly bump into something, Brian was extremely protective of his leg, he was attacked at Jennifer's. Brian grabbed his phone only to observe it was dead, he pulled himself up off the floor, and the first step on the leg dropped him to the floor again in agonizing pain. He managed to butt slide around his house to find his crutches, stood up, and crutched himself to plug in his phone. The very next task was get cleaned up. There was no way he could stand in the shower in this condition, or slide himself in or out of the bathtub, so it was cowboy wash day, brushed teeth, deodorant and cologne. Within a few minutes of his phone on the charger, he could hear his phone in the other room updating. Thankfully it was all good news from clients and friends wondering where he was and how his outing went, however there was not a single text or call from Jennifer. With the last six months to compare, his voicemail should have been full from her, likely a hundred text messages, and two hundred missed calls, but to his surprise there was absolutely nothing!

Brian needed to speak to Jennifer, this is a very serious matter, and either she is fully dominated by an entity, or her house is consumed with spirits taking over the space, her, and everyone around her. Brian knew this was the perfect opportunity for him to bail, but this thing attacked HIM, and that is just not ok! Brian has over twenty years of experience with these sorts of things, and deep within his core she needed a strong friend more then she knew it herself. Before he called, he sat and processed his approach. Brian's sixth sense is a gift, and he is an expert, but these bastards are vicious! Brian knows people in pain are the healers of the world, their wisdom flows from winning and he has helped so many, saved so many more from the ultimate sacrifice, so he confidently picked up the phone and called her. He never even heard the phone ring, he heard her start right off about how everything would still be the same had he not insisted they meet. He never got a word in for a good five minutes the speed she was talking, in different tongues and voices back and forth again as he listened to her, playing different roles of individuals waiting for the moment for himself to jump in.

Brian jumped in like breaking up a dog fight yelling *"Hey, hey, hey, hey… HEYYYYYYYYYY!"* she kept on like she never heard him, so he continued trying to butt in to get her attention. Jennifer had never been like this the entire six months showing zero aggression. Eventually he did break sequence by continually asking who Donny is?

She finally paused asking who this was? Brian said, *"Jennifer, it is Brian what's up?"* She was silent for a good twenty seconds and started back up again, he continued *"Hey, hey, hey, Jennifer… Jennifer… JENNIFER, stop I am right here."*

She responded, "What? What? WHAT!? I don't respond well to yelling, you speak to me kindly like a respectable woman, do you understand you son of a bitch!"

Patient as always, he spoke mildly, evenly, and kindly. *"Jennifer just chill and listen to me."* He could hear her breathing as if she just sprinted a mile assuring her, he can calm tense situations, and if she wanted to talk or listen. She didn't immediately respond, so he said, *"Jennifer, I think you have lost your empathy with people because for so long you have been caught up in pain as a pleasurable reward."* He said, *"For six months I have enjoyed you, what is causing all this relentless fight or flight you can't talked to me like we always have?"*

Jennifer fired right back. "I am not giving up my friends, they are all I have in this god-forsaken world."

He remained patient and calmly said, *"Jennifer, I love you, I don't care what you do for work and I would never ask you to give up your friends or change your profession, but right now you need to come back down to earth so we can talk realistically about what happened."* He reiterated calm heads prevail and until she is calm, then they shouldn't talk.

Jennifer fired right back. "So you are dumping me!?!?"

He said, *"No, not hardly, I don't give up that easily, but talking at each other is not fixing anything, something is in your house and does not like to share you—at least with me."* He asked her if she has had problems with men in her house before, and they experienced similar happenings like what happened to him.

Jennifer paused, she responded that every single male has gotten sick in her house, including relatives, repairman, friends—anyone of the male descent.

He asked again *"Who is Donny?"*

Jennifer's guard came right back up becoming very defensive and started attacking him again. She said, "You know what Brian, it is just fine, go ahead and pick on the little fat girl again. What do you want to do now, hit me"?

He fired back. *"Jennifer, I am not even there, what are you talking about or to whom?"*

Jennifer said, "I need protectors like Donny in my house to keep asshole men like you out of here... I invited you over, dressed up for you, and you call my house dirty, poke fun at me, tell me something stinks, then I am possessed, then you tried to rape me, you son of a bitch!"

Brian hung up the phone, thinking to himself whatever is in that house is twisting her brain, and before he could set the phone down it rang again. He looked at it thinking a customer was calling and it was her. He picked it up, and before he spoke, it was the little child's voice, the same one when she talks to her cats. She said, "I am sorry... please don't hate me, I am small, I love my dollies, I am going to play with them now, byeeeeeee." Click.

Again, he pondered blocking her number and bailing, but he also thought about the number of times he has dealt with the paranormal polluting humans with their infinite mind games in the many years dealing with his chronic pain. This one was making a point to mess with Brian, it was smart and very advanced, so he decided "Challenge Accepted!". After a few days he did start to miss her, remembering their daily routines, their laughs, and their beauty they shared for several months. He fell hard for this woman, and he thought how ironic he lives with chronic pain, the sixth sense, and she is a mortician with an eccentric connection with the place of pre-immortality. He knew he needed her without the influence of the spirits, so for the next couple of weeks keeping his silence he periodically received texts from her that just said, "HI." He waited a couple of hours after receiving another hi message and decided to call her and see how it went. The Jennifer he fell for was back and EXACTLY the girl he had known for several months. He couldn't help it, he fell right into the palm of her hands in love again.

She said, "Brian, I really miss you, I was selfish to treat you as I did. I was mean, I was unreasonable, I can't stop thinking about you, I love you, and whatever we have to do to get through this, I want you to know I am dedicated to whatever it takes. I completely apologize, I am asking you to forgive me. Can you do that?"

He accepted her apology, he has a general rule in life when someone asks for forgiveness, he forgives. It doesn't mean he forgets; it just means an opportunity for another chance; time will tell where the road leads. The two of them spent a couple hours on the phone like old times, they laughed, they caught up, and then she asked about his leg injury and how it works with those who have left the living world, and are now in the spiritual world.

He explained after two decades in chronic pain, combined with a genius IQ, and continual unexplained occurrences he spent endless time researching his condition to determine if he was simply losing his mind to severe pain, or the pain created a psychological condition, or there was a purpose behind it all. He told her physical pain small or large acts like an algorithm, almost like an unspoken code and disperses a two way vibration. Whoever has it, is a magnet—the more the pain the more it attracts pain seeking confirmation. He said pain is the superior power to all embodied/living things AND systematically is the ONLY vibration the disembodied seek. Jennifer asked, "So what exactly does pain and paranormal have in common"? Brian explained each person has "ONE" living spirit with twenty unique identifiers on your fingers and toes. Each fingerprint is a characteristic of significance, let's use passionate as an example. One fingerprint passionate, nineteen significant examples why an individual is passionate. Second fingerprint we will use caring, nineteen other examples why an individual is caring. Jennifer says, "I GET IT, WOW, GO ON!" Brian said, "*When pain jumps in the mix, what happens?*" Jennifer said, "pain becomes the superior power because it seeks identity!" *EXACTLY!!* Brian explained this is where the paranormal come into play because they need a body to feel too, so they stalk us, cling to us, live amongst us, and he asked her "*What is the first indication someone is feeling pain?*" Jennifer paused… she answered "crying, screams, moans, separation, tears, anger…" Brian said, "*Correct, pain is the super magnet to all paranormal so the greater the pain. it can quickly consume all of your twenty characteristics.*" Jennifer asked if there a quick solution. Brian said, "*YES… Regular cleanses!!*" Brian explained cleansings are the first and far most important thing all people can do to purify each person's personal places and spaces. Jennifer laughed and said, "Brian, I think you are making a mountain out of nothing, the only person with a problem is you, NOT ME"? They continued discussing cleansings until Jennifer began to come unhinged and defensive again about her house being dirty. Brian quickly could see where this was leading and offered happily to help her find someone to perform the service of cleansing her house of the unruly spirits and he would also happily pay the fee so the two of them could recover their relationship in a healthy manner.

Jennifer said, "What if I decline?"

Brian sternly responded "*Then, yes, I am dumping you right now and this conversation—and us—ends right here and right now.*"

Jennifer went on the defense and said she has a maid who lives right up the street and her husband comes in with her all the time, why doesn't he get sick? Brian asked if he comes in the house. At first, in a defensive tone she said, "ALL THE TIME!!" ~two minute pause~ Jennifer said now when she thinks about it the husband has only been inside her house once, she explained he carries all of her cleaning supplies on a cart and walks only to the corner of the property, and when the cleaning lady is ready to leave, the husband meets her at the same corner of the yard, and they walk home together. She became angry once again and said she was not prepared to let another stranger come into her house and perform voodoo spells in or anywhere around her house. She said, "If we are done, then we are done, Brian. FU very much." Hanging up the phone once again.

Brian's number one pet-peeve is people who hang up on him, so he let her go again, and for another month he received text messages from her again except instead of hi, she would write "The pig wants to know if you want to talk, have an oinky day!" Or, "I looked up the meaning of dirty in the dictionary, and my picture was next to it," with a follow-up text of her face. She also sent, "This is the devil calling your soul to Jennifer's," or "Hi, Brian, I am making mud pies today, I got dirty, do you think a cleansing might help me now?" Brian laughed and laughed, now this was cheap entertainment! After a while it became totally annoying, but he held his ground despite missing her. He was never going to speak to her again, and definitely never going back to her house again until she agreed to a spiritual cleansing.

By the fifth week, Brian was completely annoyed and his plan to wait her out to get the girl back was not as successful this time as it was the last time. He came to terms with differences in opinions are not something to terminate the relationship over. He gave in to at least opening the dialog again and sent her a text message that said, "Pig Shuttle #1 calling Pig shuttle #2, come in please."

Jennifer called laughing and laughing, snorting like a pig. He came right back with a different approach complimenting her on how the time in her house with her was marvelous! Jennifer's mood lightened up right away graciously thanking him and was happy he had such a nice time there. She surprised him too telling him how she had researched spiritual cleansing online and was completely open to it now. She asked him if they could talk about it more because in their last discussion the bit about the fingerprints really hit home with her, and she wanted to know more, a lot more, as much as she could! Brian was VERY happy she opened the door to enlightenment, and he knew this is where he could shine making a significant impact and he was committed to opening her up to what hides in the gray, changing her view, and working together towards the future they had always planned for.

She was intensely listening with her ear pressed tightly against the phone. Brian began with explaining more about what he learned over the last 20 years his chronic pain unveiled. He asked her if she remembers The Peanuts character, Pigpen from Charlie Brown. She said, "absolutely, but she always favored Snoopy, and Linus, but always loved how Lucy jerked the ball away from Charlie Brown, what is up with Pigpen". He said, "*All people in life have a cloud that follows them, some people call it aura. Aura is the main contributor to how people interact with each other, sometimes it is good, and sometimes bad.*" He asked her, "*Have you ever been enjoying a great day, and pass someone in crossing, and then your mood changes for no explainable reason and the rest of your day goes south?*" Jennifer excitably replied, "Two days ago I had an amazing start of the day, and I bumped into someone in passing, and the rest of the day nothing went right. I didn't know the person, but nothing went right the rest of the day."

He explained the world shows us to look up to observe the clouds are always moving above us in the skies, and when certain ones collide, we see storms, changes in the weather, it could be rain, hail, an angry storm, and beyond. Brian described his chronic pain and sixth sense combined acted almost like x-ray vision and he can see the same thing on the ground as people's clouds merge they create situations like fights, intimidation, new love, drama, breakups, injuries, illness, car crashes, etc., because the energy fogs either create storms or new beginnings. Pain being the superior power, is the ozone, it connects to all molecules of the clouds, the energy, and makes all molecules into pain. "*Aura is the main ingredient to how and why people connect or disconnect, misery loves company, and every cloud has a silver lining.*"

Jennifer was completely amazed, and said, "I am COMPLETELY mind blown right now, this is by far the most amazing conversation I have ever had, and it totally makes sense!"

He continued explaining when and where the storming clouds meet pain's ozone there is an exceptionally high amounts of sadness, regret, anger, humiliation, loss, and depression, and then following those feelings comes the possessions of the paranormal to impose revenge, hatred, envy, death, foul thoughts, injury, more pain, addiction, insomnia, etc.

Jennifer cut in again, "<u>Absolutely CORRECT!</u>"

He continued, "*When you continually are living in the fogs, it goes with you, it becomes your aura, and the more times you revisit it, it hangs on to you, and when you go home, it comes with you, when you leave home, it goes with you. Cleansing acts like a forcefield to lessen the amount of pained energies coming into your home with you and deteriorates away your life in your personal space. The more cleansing, the safer you are, because the unruly spirits are unable to enter while creating more room for you to receive love, friendship, happiness, hope, laughter, creativity, etc. to allow all good things you wish for in your life to be welcomed in.*"

She said, "Wouldn't going to church just be easier?"

He asked, "*Do you attend church?*"

Jennifer said, "Well, many of the services are held in churches, isn't that the same thing?"

He replied, "*In the twenty years I have dealt with my injury I have gone to many churches, and it is good for the soul, but churches are full of sin, and the moment you walk out of the church, your aura is still the same, you just momentarily are not thinking of it, until you re-enter the world of the clouds, thus whoever you pass, wherever you go, the same fogs attach and go with you.*"

God forbid you experience and physical pain, because you WILL be dog piled by the pained paranormal and that just adds insult to injury."

Jennifer was deep in thought, she asked "How often do you cleanse your home?"

He replied, *"As often as I need too. I have no set schedule, but homes, businesses, buildings should be cleansed once a month, quarterly at minimum, because all places where people gather the stalkers wait, and they need flushed out in order for success, peace, productivity and so on to even have a chance!"*

She asked, "How do you know when it is time?"

Brian said, *"When I come home fired up and walk inside and get even more upset, it is time for a cleansing, or when I am exhausted at home, feel down and drained after a full nights rest, it is time. Sometimes I even just sit in my car not wanting to go inside, so that would be another example for when it is time to cleanse the homestead"* He explained he also strictly follows all the guidelines of everything he has learned and tested over the last twenty years to receive the ultimate freedom from the spirits and the paranormal who continually wander amongst us all. *"Pain is the siren to call the spirits to come running, so we all must work together first and foremost staying in touch physically, be it shaking hands, hugs, talking to one another F2F, but buried in an electronic device does not count."*

He explained *"People who live in their homes always with the curtains drawn to keep the house dark, is a modern day living coffin. It is the number one indicator the individual is unknowingly collecting more spirits to come in day after day and stay. (The folklore of evil things stay out of the light is true!!) Instead keep fresh air flowing through your home, let the sunlight in, refrain from decorative bones or skulls, pictures or drawings, allow nothing to resemble dark afterlife, mutilations, evil or death, because as you bring the stalkers of your aura home, the decorations are the vacancy sign to stay at home, with you!"* *"Oh, and leave the porch light on at night, the stalkers always go to the darkness, so doing this simple task, assures they are NOT waiting at your door to come in at night when the door is opened!!"*

Jennifer said, "A large number of her suicide cases were deeply depressed people who never left their homes, is this why?"

Brian replied, "*In my opinion...* ABSOLUTELY YES!!"

CHAPTER FIFTEEN

AFTER ABOUT A WEEK OF talking, Jennifer suddenly one day started acting lost, confused, and desperate again as if she had forgotten everything they had been discussing. Jennifer said she was doing some spring cleaning at work and in the bottom of a drawer she found a photo album she kept filled with many pictures of families she got to know, and pictures of the deceased she worked with. Brian asked, *"Why are you keeping family's pictures and ones of your clients, don't those usually go home with the families, or get placed in the coffin?"* Jennifer said, "A few always get left behind, but they are for ME to remember my friends, don't you keep memories of your friends Brian?" He replied, *"So basically you keep an ongoing book of death is what you are saying?"* Jennifer wept on the phone, she continued to plea:

Brian, I know my house hasn't been cleansed, but I love my house, I only go there to sleep, my love for life is for my clients, they aren't dead to me, they are my friends, and if they want to come home with me I am ok with that. Brian your words are so profound, they make complete sense, in fact I have never heard anything more intelligent in my life, but like how you won't turn your back to me, I cannot turn my back to these peaceful people. I eat with them, I talk to them, they really listen to me, we have so much in common. I know their medical history, we enjoy so many of the same things. A woman who came in today, she was strangled to death by a stalker, and we both like the same chocolates, how can that be wrong?! I am their caretaker to take them to their final destination. It is like sending your loved ones away on a trip with all the trip snacks, immense love, best wishes, and it is my place to do this for them. Being a mortician comes naturally to me, and I can deal with my long-time problems one instance at a time. It is therapy to me, and when the one comes who looks like those who have hurt me throughout my life, I seal them in a box, bury them, it is done. Why is that wrong? With the suicides, I help them send their final message to all they wanted. I know what it is like to want to take my own life, and I take much pride and enjoy watching those assholes cry, grieve, and they absolutely deserve the pain, regret, and misery I can deliver. I come home and sleep peacefully knowing I helped another one of my friends get their message across, which they wanted to get through so clearly they were willing to die for it.

Jennifer laughed out loud and finished her plea with, "Do you think my makeup is flawless by accident?" She continued to lay it on heavily the entire process of all the practices she uses with people, even in the absolute worse circumstance. After about 45 minutes of Brian listening to her with the many gruesome details, she piped up and said, "Does any of this move you at all?"

Brian replied, "*Nope!! I have seen more than you could ever imagine. The kind of pain I live in, nothing raises my blood pressure. I know pain better than anyone. Don't you think someone with twenty-plus years of daily experience twenty-four hours a day pretty much makes me an expert?*"

Jennifer laughed. "Yes, but have you ever seen someone shot in the face, hung, drowned, dead for weeks? I can make them appear they never missed a moment in time."

He yawned out loud. "*Turn the page, what's next?*"

Jennifer said, "Brian, being a mortician is like working in a meat-packing plant. All the customer sees are the beautiful T-bone steak wrapped in plastic. Doesn't that make you want to hurl"?

"*Nope, are you trying to make me hurl? Do you want to get back to talking about the real matters, or is it my turn to see if I can make you hurl?*" This time she was laughing hysterically said she was definitely up for the challenge, because being a mortician to her, she is able to confront all of her bullies, the aggressors, face to face, the criminals who do no good, prisoners, all things from all walks of life to include all of her fears, all of her phobias, and turn them all into masterpieces.

Jennifer said, "My psychologist my parents made me go to as a child said I would never mount to anything unless I face everything I fear, including my bullies, and bury them. The way I see it, I am getting my therapy every single day. I am rewarded by the emotions of the attendants, and I bury them all six feet under. Why is this so wrong?" "Brian, I am doing a justice for myself, the deceased, and the living, because someone has to take out the trash. I get paid for it while I can bury my daily struggles, and my past, and whatever else... I can even throw my crappy lunch in the coffin and nobody would ever know!"

Brian said, "*Am I supposed to be hurling now? Because I just checked my blood pressure, and it is still normal.*"

Jennifer said angrily, "You are an asshole!"

Brian replied, "*Ok, so name me one person from your past or present who has taken the time to hear you out fully, unedited, and continued to show interest in what you are saying or doing?*"

There was a very long pause.

"Nobody, only you... But why do you even care? Wasn't getting sick and attacked enough to run you off, or are you that desperate or just plain stupid?"

"*I guess I am desperate and dumb. I get to deal with the living who are so lost they prefer making their pains everyone else's problem, just like you Jennifer because pain gets reaction. The truth is, the world is full of lonely people waiting to make an introduction. I watch the fogs and the whole other part of the population of lost and broken souls seeking identity found in expressed human emotions, ¾ makes the world bleed, and ¼ make a difference. I can pass through the fogs untouched because my pain lives in my identity, I am immune, so just call me the pain whisperer who knows everyone's secrets, and I bring them to the light.*"

"*Regular cleansings are like taking a dirty car through a car wash. When I walk into my home, I keep my spirit clean because there is no future in the past. You said it yourself, your life sucks in the regular world, you hate it and enjoy people in pain, and if you died tomorrow nobody would notice, so it is evident to me the mortician work is not working.*"

"Ok, Mister Pain Whisperer or Ghost Whisperer, who is in my house, and why?"

CHAPTER SIXTEEN

BRIAN TOLD JENNIFER, "*The spirits in her house are very possessive, and I want to help you get them out so you can return to enjoying the living world.*" He explained ghosts and spirits roaming the earth—embodied or disembodied—all have the exact same purpose in seeking continuance. Pain is a natural feeling the mind feels, it is not physical. Pain is personal, it can be mental or physical, but the mind oversees them both. Pain is also the entry way for the paranormal, so, pain the superior power, tells the mind to send alerts for help, which we all **should** run to assist. The living world mostly consumed and possessed by their own pains has turned its back on each other. When help doesn't arrive, the pain attacks all the individual twenty identities to allow the paranormal to access, by scanning which identity lacks most and latches on to it instantly to satisfy, and turn the call for help into to hate, retaliation, depression, and many others. The result is part of your new aura.

He continued, "*Everyone can do themselves a great justice by simply avoiding 3am by two hours on each end.*"

Jennifer asked, "why is that?"

Brian said, "*3am is when the disembodied spirits around the world are at their peak and very aggressively at work. Type it in your phone or computer '3am meaning', and watch what comes up*"

"BRIAN, that is EXACTLY when the MAJORITY of my clients meet death, you just totally blew my mind!!"

"So, since you know ghosts and spirits so well, then why didn't you have ninja reflexes when whatever at my house attacked you?"

"*The spirits in your house, three are younger and ineffective to me because of the strength of my pain. The fourth one is very afraid of me, it has been around a long time, and very possessive about you.*"

Brian could hear Jennifer suddenly go into a sneezing fit. She'd periodically came back to talk and start sneezing again. She said through her sneezes, "I don't know what is wrong with me, I think it is my allergies, my whole face is itching, my eyes are watering, and I can't stop sneezing."

Brian asked, "*Do you smell something really rank?*"

Jennifer said, "Yes, I am going to have to call you back, I need to throw up."

"*Get out of the house right now, take a walk, but don't hang up.*"

Jennifer was wheezing, gasping for air, sneezing repeatedly and complaining in a panic. He could hear her opening the door, locking it, she kept saying to hold on… He could hear her walking and her breathing returning to normal. Jennifer said, "Whew, I have never experienced anything like that in my house. It smelled like the sewer was backing up, I guess I need to call the plumber tomorrow."

Brian asked, "*Has this happened before?*"

She replied, "Actually NO! Not until I met you and we started talking about this stuff. What are you doing to me?"

Brian said, "*It is working, I am opening your heart, and your mind*"

He continued, "*Can you recall times where you place your keys the same place always by habit, and when it is time to go somewhere they aren't there?*

Doors open on their own, cats crying in the corner (lol)? Things that seems like common sense or a simple irregularity?"

He heard her hesitate and say, "As much as I don't want to admit it, regrettably, all of the time. You saw the cats, the Christmas tree, but I have never put anything together other than just weird cats and funky electricity. I also often see a cloudy dark swish out of the corner of my eye, but never when I look for it." She said she has been checked several times for eye problems and everything comes out normal, but sleepy or well rested, it always hangs out by one light in her front room she inherited from her grandmother. She said, "I do hear noises in the house all the time, but just figured it is the house settling, and I often have panic attacks, but thought it was long work hours." She said, "I just have strange luck, I pick the wrong men, I can't keep friends, my family never visits, so I put all of my time and energy at work because I feel much better around my dead people."

He patiently explained, "*The pain in your past remains in the present because you keep giving your pain life, and pain attracts pain. The only way to move on from the past or present pains is to cleanse them out or put up a barrier nothing can penetrate that doesn't have your best interest in mind. Paranormal feed on vulnerability. They are so intensely creative by mixing up situations to confuse you, all people begin to lose self-control. It is when the walls go up, the tears begin to flow, panic sets in, things start spinning, causing anxiety, or depression and anger. Physical pains spike the mind like salt in the wound and create even harsher doubt, and the many disabilities instilled to keep the pain brewing and multiplying to call on the fiercest, insistent, and piercing pained paranormal to swarm, pushing you to the point of no return. When the swarms are in full effect, taking over more than half of our personal identities, we feel defensive, defenseless, suffocated, and naturally fall into survival mode. It is a complete battle within us between mind and body. The first thought is how to reach a comfort zone to cope the quickest way possible, which is pain into pleasure most commonly through substances, and if the paranormal has already reached possession status, addiction is the learned solution."*

Jennifer fired back, "I bet you are going to tell me I need Jesus, because I am going to tell you right now, I don't believe in God or Jesus. I don't believe in any of that malarkey!"

Brian said, "*Have you ever heard the old saying, a snake never crosses a braided rope?*

She said, "Yes, I have heard that, it goes something like, if you are camping snakes can crawl in your sleeping bag to find warmth, but if you put a braided rope around you on the ground they will never cross it. Right?"

Brian said, "*Exactly! Over the years, when faced with the most intense physical and mental pains combined with being swarmed by the most insane and persistent pained paranormal, the thought of suicide entered my mind a few times.*"

Jennifer was very intense and insistently asked, "Okay… so how does this pertain to the rope theory?"

He replied, "*In all of the disembodied world there are two words that, no matter what, even if you don't believe, create the braided rope barrier. All spirits—small, large, intense, demons, ghouls, devil, phantoms—it is impossible for them to penetrate, go around, nothing, it is an instant forcefield, and it works consistently every single time. I have had plenty of time to perfect it all, test it, and to cleanse, use the barrier words, and doing the bare minimums of avoiding the 3am hour like the plague, it is like removing a stain, and the ghosts and spirits start to realize there is nothing there, nothing to grab on to, so they get bored and move on. The alternative is don't do anything and the energy gets blown back into the unruly bad spirits and starts all over again, except they come back with a vengeance, so the only way to take control, is make you lose control and let them take you over for their needs.*"

Jennifer said, "I am back at home, I feel disoriented, I got cold, I am very tired, and it is getting late." She was not willing to listen or talk anymore, or hear the end of the braided rope theory, so they said goodnight and hung up.

CHAPTER SEVENTEEN

JENNIFER WAS QUIET THE ENTIRE next day, Brian did not push the subject, he knew he needed to wait on her until she was ready. At 8pm on the dot she rang. She was very emotional and pretty tipsy! She said "Brian, you were right about drinking to feel pleasure from pain, I was so down and depressed all day, so I came home and said F it, but now I am out of alcohol, can you go get me more, you might get lucky?" He asked her *"what is going on, why the mid-week drinks, that isn't like you."* He listened to her for more than an hour talking about many different subjects extroverting her ideals and conclusions about what happened after they hung up the night before. This was the first time Jennifer had ever spoken to Brian directly without using second or third person, changing subjects, combined with different voices... She was truly one-on-one with him. She was tipsy, but concerned, scared and directly explaining what happened when she suddenly had to hang up the night before.

When Jennifer got home last night, the door was hard to push open. When she finally got it open enough to peep her head in to see what was blocking the door from opening, she watched her two cats scurry into hiding spots, and the Christmas tree was knocked over laying in front of the door. She described many pictures were on the floor, a laundry basket appeared to have tumbled all the way down the stairs, tossing laundry everywhere, and she described this was the first time ever in her own home she felt fear. She said she pulled the door shut, walked back out to the end of her property and called the police to report a break-in. Jennifer said her common sense would say the cats jumped on top of the laundry bag, tumbling down the stairs, hit the tree, knocking it over in the path of the door, unplugging it, popping the breakers, and this is what occurred.

What changed her theory and made her opt to call the police, was she did one load of laundry two days ago, and the rest of the clothes were still in the laundry basket downstairs in the laundry room and the door was still closed to the laundry room when she came in after the police searched to get some belongings.

She said, "Brian, the clean clothes were still hung up in the laundry room!!"

She described when the police arrived, they went to the breaker box first, and multiple breakers were popped. The police searched her home for intruders to find nothing, so they waited with her to pack a bag, and recommended she stay with friends tonight or in a nearby hotel. Jennifer said she called out from work today, and when she came in her house to investigate, the china hutch door housing her grandmother's dishes, the door was open, and it has not been opened on that side for as long as she could remember. She said she just lost it, crying, and went straight to a local bar for drinks.

She yelled, "Brian, why now?" "It is all exactly what you described, said... Everything about the unexplained occurrences, the odor... What are you doing to me?"

He said, "*Nothing, I simply opened you up to my world, just as you opened your world to me. Do you want to run away now, just as you couldn't understand why I didn't run away from you?*"

Jennifer finally had hit bottom and asked him to tell all. She was a sponge now and wanted a better life.

He explained, *The pained spirits have made you believe the living are the enemy and separated you from all others to the point you have no compassion or empathy for anyone but the lifeless deceased. This is exactly how the pained paranormal work, to divide us all away from one another. They don't want you feeling anything but pain, and the only way to identify pain is embodiment to give pain identity. Pain is the superior power, it is personal to everyone. The more the pain the more it closes off the world, and it keeps you away from any opportunities of self-perseverance, new beginning, healing, and growth. Instead, pain robs you, causes loss of identity, loneliness, hatred, uncertainty, creates acts of cruelty, anger, jealousy, harm, revenge, trauma, suspicion…a long list of things.*

"*Look how it has run everyone in your life away, won't let anyone into your beautiful home, convinced you your only purpose in life is to continue sending the message of pain, sadness, and suffering, even in death to family, friends, strangers, and innocent bystanders. The pained paranormal have imbued you—crying, sadness, regret, anguish, and distress are your obligation, and the more of it you can create, is your reward, recognition, and tribute to the point anything resembling happiness, delight, or bliss is wrong.*

She said, "Brian, you are so right. To see anyone upbeat in any way, I feel threatened, belittled, bullied, and hatred… And when anyone asks me for a favor or to do anything for them, I purposely don't because I prefer others upset. I just feel better that way." She paused. "So you are telling me the more I like seeing others in pain is fueling a possession or possessions I have?"

"*Yep!*"

Jennifer was totally stuck for words, stuttering, before she began verbally attacking Brian once again, then trying to excuse herself to get back to work because many others are waiting on her who like her just the way she is.

He said, "*I like you just the way you are!!*"

Jennifer paused and yelled again "You are such a jerk!!"

Brian said, "*I thought we were just talking, do you want to talk?*"

She said, "No, goodbye," and hung up!

CHAPTER EIGHTEEN

THE NEXT DAY JENNIFER CALLED with an apology, she was afraid for the first time in as long as she could remember. She heard, smelled, saw so many things it would put the movie *The Conjuring* to shame. She said she couldn't sleep, had nightmares all night, tossed and turned, anxiety, sad, and shamed him extensively for uprooting her purpose in life, and agreed to cleansing her house. Finally!!

Both of them went to work immediately with their laptops open, talking on the phone about it, and within an hour, they got lucky! Between the two of them, they found one, and he had an opening and could come right over the next day at 2pm. Brian told Jennifer he would also be over to her house for the first time since the attack to wait outside with her for the cleanser to show up, and help however he could. The next day Brian arrived about 1:15pm and Jennifer was sitting out front waiting. When Brian exited his car from the street, she went over to greet him, and Brian held his hand out to her at about twenty feet away and said, *"Not yet, let's get this done. I can see and feel it from here."*

Jennifer was very offended, he could see in her a fear like a young child, full of anxiety, confusion, and indecisiveness. Within ten minutes an old car pulled up the street, he could see it was Plymouth, about 1950, looks like an old Cambridge, green, slowly riding up the street and he could see the man inside looking for address markings. Brian waived his arms over his head back and forth, and the driver flashed his headlights signaling contact was made. Was it the cleanser? Jennifer said she had never seen this car on her street before and looked on to have a glimpse of history driving up the road. As the old car pulled in right in front of her house, the man in the car was writing something down, probably his mileage or arrival time. As the man exited his car, they both saw a pretty frail looking thin man. (Brian guessed in his mind he must have been between 65-70) He was dressed like a priest, exactly like something you would see in a movie, and in a southern accent said, "I am looking for Jennifer and or Brian." Brian smiled and reached out to shake his hand, and the old man reached out a cool soft hand giving a firm hand shake in return. Brian turned to introduce Jennifer as she stood with her arms folded, and said to Brian "This is your idea, you deal with it."

Brian responded to the man in full utter respect for being a priest and a senior citizen, he said, "*Hello, Father, I am Brian, thank you for coming out on such short notice.*" The old man obliged also very respectfully, Brian could sense and feel this old man was pure, he felt right. Brian did not tell the old man Jennifer was an active mortician, he only explained he is a long-time sufferer of chronic pain and had a sense of something unfriendly in the home. The frail old man responded, "I am very familiar with spirits like this who stalk people in pain, they are intelligent critters, but I can help you". The old man informed Brian and Jennifer he needed about an hour in the house, and the fee would be $500 dollars for the entirety of his service on that day.

Brian said, "*Father, I will happily pay you after the service, just like I do the plumber or lawn service guys. You should always pay for a job well done to show appreciation, correct?*"

The old man smiled, placed his hand on Brian as a gesture of respect and appreciation and said, "Of course, my son, no problem, but you do know tipping is not a city in China, right?"

Brian and the old man chuckled together, the old man was very genuine and fair. Jennifer stood watching on with a very concerned look on her face. The old man graciously walked back over to his car, and Jennifer snickered talking in a loud whisper, "He is gonna leave, and that is the worst god-awful fake costume I have ever seen, this is so stupid. It is your money Brian; I hope this makes you happy!" Brian said, "*Just give the guy a chance and let's see what happens, he does have a cool car, and he came over on short notice.*"

The priest went to the trunk of his car, opened it, and pulled out a finely-strapped wide, dark-brown alligator-skinned suitcase with brass buckles. Brian the antique enthusiast had not seen one like that in a long time, it was probably 1930-1940 era. The old man sat the case on the ground, fixed his collar, put on a crucifix, and started chanting. He continued chanting as he walked from the car, passed Brian stopping to bless him, paused…, and then asked if he could go ahead and walk inside. Brian looked to Jennifer and said, "*Jennifer, this is your home, and in order for this to work correctly, YOU have to provide permission.*" Jennifer with haste, waived the old man onward giving him permission to enter. The old man also stopped in front of Jennifer and blessed her also, continuing his chant as he approached the front door. The old man blessed the front door, he then opened the security door, opened the front door, walked in, closing both doors behind himself. It wasn't fifteen seconds and Jennifer and Brian heard the front door open again, and the old man walked right back out of the house as if he forgot something. The old man was so white in the face, he had that same greenish tint to him Brian had, and his eyes were wide open. The old man completely exited, walked slowly no longer chanting, and said, "THAT is way over my head, but I know someone stronger," and kept walking right past Brian and Jennifer never stopping until he got to his car. When he opened the trunk this time, he was so disoriented he even hit himself in the head so hard it was likely heard a block away, but it never even phased him. He threw the suitcase in the trunk, went around to the driver's door, got in, started the car holding the starter down way too long grinding the starter. He hit the starter a few more times with the car running which Brian knew this was due the entity in Jennifer's house who attacked him, also attacked the old man. Still disoriented the old man put the old car in reverse, slammed on the brakes, put the car in forward, slammed on the brakes again, same thing in reverse again, slammed on the brakes for a third time, and finally for the last time back in drive going forward, and sped away. It was very clear and evident to Brian he saw "it" or "them." The man didn't make a U-turn or anything, he just drove straight in a way to get out of there as quickly as possible. Brian did try to call the old man and no answer, it went straight to voicemail.

Jennifer said, "Oh, great, see, Brian, see, I am a disease!"

Brian replied, "*Just stop, that car wasn't cheap, could be a blessing in disguise, but we are not giving up!*"

Jennifer mocked, "So where is your braided rope now?"

He paused and said, "*That reminds me, we never finished that conversation, about the braided rope & the snake, and how 'my' custom braided rope works every single time without a single flaw or fail.*" Brian explained "*When I discovered it, I tested it endlessly, I have had countless opportunity, subjects, circumstances, around the clock, even when I sleep to test it, and it never failed even once, it absolutely works 100% of the time!*" She was beyond curious and asked him to continue. Brian said, "*I say rope, but it is actually the use of 2 words, but a short and quick trick is required after each use to keep it refreshed and ready with endless use, and ready to go at all times."*

Jennifer asked "what is the trick to recharge it? New batteries?"

He said, "*It is simple, just give it praise, and say thanks, & voila, recharged*"

Jennifer was now laughing again and like always, she said, "What are you going to say, your mystery fibers are God or Jesus, or both?"

Brian said, "*Yup, using the words God and Jesus is automatic protection. It works instantly every single time like water is to a flame, like soap is to dirt, it is an automatic forcefield causing instant solutions, and the spirits are bound by it.*"

Jennifer said, "Brian, I don't believe in God or Jesus, so try again."

Brian said, "*You don't have to believe in it, and neither did I for a long time, but the more times than I can count I have been in peculiar situations, full-on paranormal attack, anxiety, spinning, intense unexplained occurrences, the fogs, black shadow figures, and said, 'Papa G and JC protect me now,' and it changed the circumstances within seconds. I also follow the rules about 3am, and the other things we have discussed after the last seven to eight months. Trust me, it is a very fast solution, it just requires the recharge, and as it keeps working, and so does your usage, it WORKS!!*"

Still laughing, Jennifer said, "So you expect me to walk around and say GJ this, GJ that? No, that is just unnecessary."

He asked, "Have you ever tried it?"

She said, "Let me try… God and Jesus, or GJ or JG or Papa G & JC, I command you to tell Brian it is time to go home now."

Brian replied, "*See how good that works? I am leaving now, bye.*" and *left!*

CHAPTER NINETEEN

FOR THE NEXT COUPLE OF weeks Jennifer and Brian spoke less and less, and the times they tried it was very unnatural, nothing that hadn't been said already, she wasn't budging, just the continual victim and mocking Brian every time they spoke. Brian continued to try to convince her otherwise, tried to continually lift her up, tried finding another cleaner, but mostly things between the two of them continued to deteriorate.

The two of them had not talked, exchanged text messages for two months, then three months, then four months passed without a single communication, until one day.... Jennifer called Brian. He was just not in the mood, the relationship was dead, and knowing her passion to create horror, he was not about to give her a chance, or maybe it was a butt-dial. He let the phone ring right into voicemail. Then he received a text message and it said, "Yes, I called you on purpose, pick up please." Brian did not respond, but something was different this time... she wasn't obsessively calling, no crazy lady texts and calls, but rather fifteen minutes she called again. Against his better judgement he answered and said, "*What's up?*"

Jennifer was bubbly as usual, not at all salty, so very excited about something, and her stuttering unable to barely mumble out she said, "Oh my god, oh my god, you are totally going to freak out when I tell you what happened to me today."

Brian was very weary, but he said, "*Go ahead, I am listening.*"

She said, "One of my colleagues, who is also a mortician, asked me last week if I ever do spiritual cleansings, and of course I thought of you, Brian."

"*Ok, so you called me to tell me I was right, or scold me again? Why did you call?*"

Jennifer said, "Are you sitting down? Brian, you were right, and you are never going to believe what my girlfriend said after she cleansed my house, and who was in it."

He replied, "*Whatever, Jennifer, this is just another one of your games. I have heard this for almost a year now, just get to the punchline.*"

Jennifer said, "Brian, you were 100% correct, there were exactly four spirits in my house!! The old person is my grandmother, my friend said she is connected all over my house to several items, however the dishes in my china cabinet were her pride and joy, and her strongest strengths resided there. The smells were her, she attacked you because she doesn't like you. In fact, she likes no men around me at all, probably because my bullies were men growing up and my dad was mean to me. My girlfriend said, 'This guy Brian is amazing and you should listen to him, he knows what he is talking about, your grandmother tried her best in attacking him using the odors, making him sick, grabbing his injury, because she felt he was trying to run her off, so she viciously attacked him."

Jennifer continued, explaining besides the grandmother, two more of the spirits in her house were young children whose deaths occurred during the holiday season, both belonging to the same father, and she prepared the children to always be remembered as children of God through the Christmas season. Jennifer said her girlfriend reiterated taking a personal discourse with the father and taking care of the children with immense care, more than their mother did, the children attached to Jennifer and her grandmother for protection. The last and final spirit in her house was a teenage boy who was harshly bullied. Jennifer also connected with him on a very deep emotional level, so the boy connected with Jennifer, and the other spirits in her house seeking love and safety. Jennifer said the girlfriend reinforced that a mortician's duty is a celebration versus a reason to send everlasting messages of pain and suffering. She said, "Brian, she also spoke of pain is the superior power just like you did, and too much connection to pain and suffering, death and dying, negativity, depression, anxiety is where a higher equivalence of the world resides". The girlfriend said a mortician's duty is to suppress pain, build empathy, a time of blessings, togetherness, new beginnings, and support. We all have an unknown expiration, but we all need each other to cope, and togetherness keeps the unruly spirits confused unable to attach to multiples, because possessions occur one on one, so keep helping one another, cleanse regularly keeps them at a minimum. The girlfriend said, "this guy is an earth angel, his theory of GJ rope is the most beautiful, wonderful thing she has ever heard, and by far the most powerful and worthy use of protection. This guy crossing your path is a modern-day miracle!!"

Jennifer said, "Are you happy now?"

Brian replied, "*Yes, but how do you know if the cleansing worked, and everyone is gone?*

She said in a cocky voice, "Well.... I can unplug the Christmas tree and all the lights stay on."

Brian laughed like he hadn't for ages! His heart was full, another miracle, and another win! He sat and listened to Jennifer chatterbox away about how she was going to take all the Christmas decorations down, repaint her house, rearrange her house, and all her many plans.

She was a completely different person than the one he met. She said her girlfriend mixed up a special elixir in a one-gallon container she pours into a spray bottle and placed protection items around the house in the areas the most pronounced activities occur. Every time she leaves the house, she uses the solution to spray herself with a fine mist, and when she comes home before she enters the house, she also mists herself. In addition, once a month her girlfriend will come over to refill her bottle of solution and cleanse her house to ensure Jennifer will be able to live a happy and fulfilling life. Jennifer told Brian she even uses the words Papa G and JC when she feels uncertainty, and it is working, she is full, she is happy, and she is free! She apologized in length for anything and everything, harm, vulgarity, accusations, a long list and thanked him for saving her life, her sanity, and will forever be thankful for his genuine generosity, and not giving up on her.

CONCLUSION

LIFE IS WHAT YOU MAKE it, but it is imperative to spend a few moments each day for self-reflection, wash away your pains, remember your GJ rope in emergency moments, and always save room for dessert. Living in the past is living in pain in the present. This life of embodiment was given as an opportunity to change the direction of your spirit before it returns to a disembodied state to continue its spiritual journey. Always be empathetic and compassionate to others. Your twenty unique identities are yours, and yours only, but can easily be consumed by the superior power of pain. The answers to your pain also lay within your identities. When in doubt, look at the top ten identities on the tips of your fingertips to remind you how special, unique, and wonderful you really are, and show all whom you meet just how spiritually upright you are.

Final Quote:

"God's fiercest warriors fight the toughest battles."

SIX-YEAR UPDATE

BRIAN: IN NOVEMBER OF 2015, Brian received his eighteenth leg surgery of a complete leg reconstruction from the knee down, he is healing well. He reports he has a playful curious spirit who visits regularly to his home, named Jack. The spirit loves to play hide and seek and is of child descent. Brian's sixth sense is still very strong, and he actively continues to educate others and help them find their potential through using pain for success. He does some life coaching and is continuing to write more books. Brian also met a strong Christian woman, and plan on getting married.

Jennifer: Just two years after the conclusion of this story reached out to Brian to report she met a new man. She admitted to stopping the cleansings, and the new man also fell very ill in the same way Brian did, and fled the house and never spoke to her again. Brian advised Jennifer as he did before, and she complained she didn't want to spend the money on cleansings. The girlfriend out of good faith did return to perform another cleanse. She reported a new group of spirits entered her home, along with grandma, but this time much more resistive, and Jennifer refuses to keep up with regular cleanses, and finds her passion in her clients and the deceased, but performs her profession sending a good message and lives amongst the spirits single. Jennifer was seen a year ago on a social interview back into the singles scene looking to meet someone.

Dedicated to Alfred:

Always Live for Respect Every Day

The End